The

CHAMPIONSHIP
FORMULA

{ *How to Transform Your*
Team Into a Dynasty }

JACK STARK, Ph.D.

The

CHAMPIONSHIP
FORMULA

{ *How to Transform Your*
Team Into a Dynasty }

JACK STARK, Ph.D.

EMERALD
BOOK CO.

Published by Emerald Book Company
Austin, TX
www.emeraldbookcompany.com

Copyright ©2012 Jack Stark, Ph.D.

Distributed by Emerald Book Company

For ordering information or special discounts for bulk purchases, please contact Emerald Book Company at PO Box 91869, Austin, TX 78709, 512.891.6100.

Design and composition by Greenleaf Book Group LLC
Cover design by Greenleaf Book Group LLC

Publisher's Cataloging-In-Publication Data
(Prepared by The Donohue Group, Inc.)
Stark, Jack A., 1946-
  The championship formula : how to transform your team into a dynasty / Jack Stark. — 1st
    ed.
    p. ; cm.
  ISBN: 978-1-937110-01-7
  1. Coaching (Athletics) 2. Teamwork (Sports) 3. Leadership. I. Title.
GV711 .S72 2012
796.077   2011932965

Part of the Tree Neutral® program, which offsets the number of trees consumed in the production and printing of this book by taking proactive steps, such as planting trees in direct proportion to the number of trees used: www.treeneutral.com

Printed in the United States of America on acid-free paper

11 12 13 14 15 16   10 9 8 7 6 5 4 3 2 1

First Edition

Dedication to Our Family

TO JOHN,

Who taught so many how to live life despite his severe
disability and who remains an inspiration to us all.

TO NICK,

Who teaches us how to work hard through all
his sacrifice. We are incredibly proud of you.

TO SUZY,

Who teaches us how to have passion and
resilience in pursuit of her dream. God bless you.

TO SHIRLEY,

Who teaches us how to love and who dedicated
her life to each of us. A remarkable woman.

We have been truly blessed!

Contents

Introduction

It is a rough road that leads to the heights of greatness.
—Lucius Annaeus Seneca

It was the worst day of my life! A day that I will never forget.

It was a day that would test me.

That day would determine who and what I would be.

What decision would I make? I wanted to quit—I did not think I could make it.

It was that defining moment when I realized that if I was going to be successful in life, I had to persevere. I must possess the character of a leader.

What guided my decision that night, November 11, 1972, was my experience a decade earlier.

It was a lazy spring day in the Midwest in 1962. I was running a timed lap at track practice. I wasn't very good at long-distance running and really not that motivated as a high school sophomore.

I started out the lap fast but quickly faded and jogged the last fifty yards.

Then it happened!

Out of nowhere, my all-sport coach, Dick Kutlas, a calm person whom I greatly admired, immediately came over to me after observing my behavior. I did not realize that it was a "really big deal" to him.

After all, I was his starting quarterback in football and had a special relationship with him. But he knew instantly that if we as a team and I as its potential leader were going to be successful, such behavior was unacceptable.

His words are forever embedded in my soul. He grabbed me by the shirt with both fists and looked me straight in the eyes and said, "You listen and you listen good! I don't care if you have to crawl across that finish line, but you'd better finish. Do you hear me?" Shocked and dazed, I said, "Yes, Coach."

I was startled but not totally surprised. He was a great teacher. He was a leader who cared enough about me to teach me. I tucked his words away in my mind and never once thought about them for the next decade. I moved on without realizing the impact they would have on my life.

Flash forward to 1972. My first son was born on July 30 of that year, a perfectly healthy baby. And now, just three months later, I was sitting at the nursing station of the Pediatric Intensive Care Unit at our local hospital.

I was in a fog, as I had averaged only two hours' sleep each night over the previous five days. Our only child, John, was just three months old and terribly sick. We had taken him to our family doctor four days earlier and were assured he would be okay—it was just the flu. Just give him baby aspirin and Jell-O water.

I have often wondered whether, if my mind had been more focused, things would have turned out so tragically.

I was also about to take the biggest test of my life—my doctoral exams.

The tests were to be administered over five days beginning November 13, ten hours each day, over five major areas of psychology.

I had studied for six straight months and had charted over six hundred study hours. If I flunked, then I would be out of the program, my career as a psychologist over.

The tests were to start on Monday, and here I was on a Saturday night at the hospital.

The general practitioner had a difficult time drawing spinal fluid from our son, who was listless by that time. When the doctor saw how cloudy the spinal fluid was, he called in a specialist—but by then, it was too late.

The pediatrician rushed in and instantly knew how bad it was. He told us that our son had meningitis and was seriously ill. I could tell that he was very concerned that we could lose him. As I sat in shock, I picked up a medical textbook at the nurse's station and read about the possible consequences that he had discussed with us. It mentioned visual and auditory impairment and, most disturbing, mental retardation, an area I was working in at the time.

It was the darkest, most depressing moment of my life. I wanted to quit. How could I possibly take this difficult test, with little sleep and with my son in the ICU clinging to life?

Then it happened! I actually heard my coach's voice. Out of nowhere, I clearly heard his words—"You listen and you listen good! I don't care if you have to crawl across that finish line, but you'd better finish."

Somehow I got through that week. I don't know how I did it other than by knowing I had to finish no matter what.

Had I dropped the test, I probably would have dropped out of the program and had an entirely different career and life.

Coach's words also guided my behavior with my family as we took care of our severely disabled son for the thirty years he was with us.

There would be many more challenges over my career, points at which I wanted to quit, but as coach taught me, that's not what a leader does.

Perhaps these experiences have driven my quest in finding the answer to the question "What makes a great leader, particularly a leader who can build a great team or company that lasts so long that it can be labeled a dynasty?"

Answering that question is the purpose of this book.

THE NEED FOR A DYNASTY

A dynasty can be defined by the success and longevity of an entity. A country, civilization, company, organization, or team that so dominates its time—whether for centuries or decades—can earn this label. The complexity of the world today, however, increases the difficulty of sustaining success.

People want answers. Today a Fortune 500 CEO can expect to keep that job for 3.6 years, and for head coaches at the professional level, it's only 4.6 years. Why? Why is it so difficult both to win and to win consistently? And why is it so difficult to win long enough to sustain a "dynasty"? And why is it even more difficult to be the most dominant entity of an era?

Perhaps "big expectations due to big bucks" explains it. Bidding for both top corporate management and sports stars is everywhere—see salaries for CEOs at Goldman Sachs and Blackrock Financial and coaches for Kentucky basketball teams, Alabama football teams, or the Lakers and the Yankees.

Where to start?

There are more than a thousand books written worldwide each year on businesses and sports teams seeking to become dynasties. Over one hundred of those books touch specifically on the issues of leadership and teamwork. So why another book on this topic—what is so unique or different to warrant your attention? There are lots of interesting stories about the success and failure of companies and teams, but rarely are they verified or grounded in a model and theory as to why they work—beyond the "this is what we did."

Whatever your occupation or interest, in business or in sports, you probably enjoy reading stories of success and learn a few things in each of the books you read. Then you want to take this insight and apply it to your own situation in order to increase your winning percentages and ROI. You want a winning formula—a formula that is easy to understand and implement.

In this book I provide that winning formula. It is an integrated model based upon research theory grounded in successful outcomes over an eighty-year period. This theory demonstrates how this model can be successfully applied to the construction of a championship team that develops into a dynasty over time. I have been fortunate to observe this model applied to some of our top Fortune 500 companies and the teams I have consulted with who have won their respective national championships. I have attempted to present research findings that are backed by a lifetime of experience and applied to what worked, how it worked, why it worked, and when and by whom the model for success was implemented.

THE CREATION OF A DYNASTY

The financial meltdown of 2008–2010 (which saw the downfall of Lehman Bros., Bear Stearns, Wachovia, and Washington Mutual) and the firing of coaches with 9–3 records (e.g., Solich at Nebraska in 2003) have changed the rules. Patience is gone and the pressure to produce immediately is enormous. I experienced this process with one of the most remarkable men I have ever met—Tom Osborne, currently athletic director at Nebraska and former head coach with 255 wins in twenty-five years.

I clearly recall a conversation with Coach Osborne after a "bad" season of 9–3 in 1990. We came off a big bowl loss and I went to Coach with a plan for team unity. He asked me if it would work. I said, "Coach, it will work pretty well the first year, and by the third or fourth year we could win a championship." I will never forget his response—it was typical of a true winner. I expected that he would be elated at my timetable. NO! Instead, he looked at me sternly and said, "Jack, you don't understand— this is football and we have to win now—right now!" We had dropped to a really low level of twenty-third in the national rankings. We implemented a program (Unity Council) and within three years had come close to a national championship, only barely losing on the last play of the game (a field goal miss against Florida State). But we went on a 60–3 run over the next five years, 1993–1997, with three national championships. We were the most dominant team of the 1990s, with an 86–11–1 record—the definition of a dynasty.

How did we do it, and how can others do it? Popular books are quickly outdated as top coaches are fired and as "too big to fail" companies fail. All this has occurred in the last ten years. So what happened? We were led to believe that these companies and teams were "built to last." Leadership gurus had high praise for the incredible success of Enron, Tyco, Lehman Bros., etc., etc. and these companies were selected as business leaders of the year by various publications. Then we found out it was all a fraud.

HOW TO SUSTAIN A DYNASTY

The global interconnectedness and demand for transparency will challenge every leader in his or her goal of developing a winning record over a consistent period of time.

We can learn much from the companies and teams who have built dynasties—Berkshire Hathaway, Apple, McDonald's, Microsoft, and the UCLA and Lakers teams.

The past rules of success no longer work. Added to that is the realization that some of what we thought was working was really a huge fraud, giving us Madoff and Enron.

THE "GOOD TO GREAT" FAILURE

In 2001 we thought we had the answer in Jim Collins's book *Good to Great*. We were told that "good" is the enemy of "great"! But it turned out that "great" wasn't so great after all.

His research was impressive. He reviewed 1,435 companies that appeared on the Fortune 500, and only eleven companies were able to meet his criteria of delivering at least three times the general stock market average over a fifteen-year period ranging from 1964 to 1998. So what happened in the last decade, 2000–2010? My analysis is shown in the following table.

COMPANY	PROFITS	PERIOD	OUTCOME 2000–2010
1. Abbott	4 x Market	1974–1989	4 x market via acquisitions & debt. *Criteria met.*
2. Circuit City	18.5 x Market	1982–1997	Bankrupt in January 2009. *Criteria not met.*

COMPANY	PROFITS	PERIOD	OUTCOME 2000–2010
3. Fannie Mae	7.5 x Market	1984–1999	TARP bailout. Lost 7 x Market. Massive losses. *Criteria not met.*
4. Gillette	7.4 x Market	1980–1995	Acquired by P&G in 2005. *Criteria not met.*
5. Kimberly-Clark	3.4 x Market	1972–1987	2 x market. *Criteria not met.*
6. Kroger	4.2 x Market	1973–1978	2 x market. *Criteria not met.*
7. Nucor	5.2 x Market	1975–1990	7 x market. Massive debt taken on via acquisition. *Criteria met.*
8. Philip Morris	7.1 x Market	1964–1979	Changed company (Altria to Philip Morris International) via acquisition and buyout. *Criteria not met.*
9. Pitney Bowes	7.2 x Market	1973–1988	Lost money—2 x market. *Criteria not met.*
10. Walgreens	7.4 x Market	1975–1990	2 x Market. *Criteria not met.*
11. Wells Fargo	4 x Market	1983–1998	TARP bailout. *Criteria not met.*

The outcomes are shocking! Only two of the eleven companies maintained the success criterion of showing at least three times the average stock market earnings. TARP bailouts, bankruptcy, acquisition, and inability to maintain earnings level characterize all the others. The successful two took on debt and grew only by acquisition. It remains to be seen whether they can sustain their success.

So what happened and why? It turns out that these companies had Level 5 leaders (the level of leaders Collins defined on a 5–1 level with five being the highest), but it's a bit more complicated than Collins's description of these five levels.

THE PSYCHOLOGY OF FAILURE VS. HOPE

There is a whole new way for failed or fired CEOs to make money and get attention. It's called "How I got fired and failed and what you can do to avoid it." Guess what? It's working. Ever go to a workshop and note that the failed exec's talk is packed? TV interviews, news articles, and books have fed this new obsession. Years ago these individuals went off and hid—often with their big buyout bucks. Perhaps it's a psychological survival-of-the-fittest phenomenon. "It's so complicated out there today that I don't know what to do, Jack, but at least I now know what not to do, in order to get by." That's what I hear from many leaders today.

Hope gets us excited about the future, but worrying about failure protects us from being overly optimistic in the present. Research tells us that, as humans, we are predisposed to pay great attention to the negative. This is an evolutionary protection. Paying attention to a saber-toothed tiger's threat comes before paying attention to rewards. Hope, however, brings about a special kind of happiness that is longer-lasting. Leaders of teams need to inspire hope but always remain vigilant of what causes failure and what could pull a team apart—it can happen quickly.

TEAM-TO-DYNASTY TIP #1. It is four times harder and takes four times as long to build a successful dynasty than to destroy one.

WHY TEAMS FAIL

In his book *The Five Dysfunctions of a Team*, Patrick Lencioni describes in a fable format why he thinks teams—even the best ones—often struggle. Based on his own perceptions rather than empirical research, he lists trust, conflict, commitment, accountability, and a focus on results as key ingredients to success. While all these traits are factors, they miss the main reasons.

My experience and research show that companies fail mainly because of greed and arrogance. There is so much money on the line today—hundreds of millions of dollars for CEOs, $4 to 10 million for head coaches. Leaders today often make more money in one day than their parents made in their lifetime—this is a game changer!

This opportunity raises expectations and leads to more leaders being tempted to cut corners. Think of BP's oil spill!

Leonard Sayles and Cynthia Smith, in *The Rise of the Rogue Executive: How Good Companies Go Bad and How to Stop the Destruction* point out that Enron CEO Jeff Skilling—serving jail time for his part in the stunning bankruptcy of this one-time top energy company—graduated from Harvard Business School in the top 5 percent of his class. Yet he was described by his peers as arrogant and out of touch with reality.

At Home Depot and Chrysler, Bob Nardelli, so successful at GE, failed terribly as the CEO because he stubbornly refused to understand the culture of these companies, and his command-and-control tactics of ramming through his ideas alienated key managers. Those managers left, resulting in his demise.

Another former GE guy, Daniel Mudd, lost millions and needed a government bailout for Fannie Mae. After being forced out in 2008, he admitted that he needed to learn to be more humble.

AIG (American International Group) needed a $182 billion federal bailout and traced much of that damage in its financial products division to Joe Cassano's leadership (2001–2008).

PURPOSE OF THE BOOK

It has been said that leadership is an "all-the-time thing." It is sometimes demanding and lonely at the top. However, knowing not only what works, but also why teams fail—examining the records of companies and sports teams who have long dominated their fields and then failed—will help us to understand how dynasties are built. Remember the words of the great warrior Sun Tzu: "Know yourself and know others"—"others" referring to enemies or competition.

We thought we had some answers in the 1980s and 1990s about leaders and what the magic formula was for success. Then in the past decade, from 2000 to 2010, all that changed. The new "new" of winning leadership and success in companies and teams has forever changed. The demand for transparency and accountability and our ability to see leadership behavior in the national media require a more comprehensive explanation that specifies the who, what, why, where, and how of building a lasting and successful enterprise. That's the purpose of this book.

THE MODEL

Breakthrough thinking hit me accidentally early in my career. It jumped off the pages of an old book as I was researching social service programs. The missing puzzle piece I had been looking for was an explanation of why the billions of dollars spent on human service programs had such little positive impact. As I had observed, most social service programs came and went based on the latest flavor-of-the-month approach or what I call "leadership by best seller." There was no unifying model or theory to explain why some programs are successful and others are not.

Blue Cross Since 1929: Accountability and the Public Trust (1975), by Oden W. Anderson, is the obscure and seldom-read book that rocked my thinking. It is based on social-psychology theory and research. Reading it gave me the key that unlocked the "dynasty formula model" in my mind.

Dr. Anderson was a sociology professor at the University of Michigan and later at the University of Chicago. His frame of reference and background was in social-political-economic movements. His experiences led him to understand that there is a latent division of labor that every successful company and team needs in order to have long-term success. The longevity of Blue Cross Blue Shield and its impact on health care all over the world are a tribute to this "division of labor" model. In this book, published in 1975 and now out of print, Anderson traces how health-care delivery developed in the United States. Subsequently many other places in the world adopted the model. The delivery system has now been in effect for more than seventy-five years.

When I came across Anderson's research, I instantly realized how this explains (1) who the core people in a company or on sports team must be, and (2) what is required to win championships and become a dynasty. In other research and experiences I discovered a process of building or maintaining a dynasty congruent with one's purpose in life.

In this book, I map out how this model is the underlying common factor in each successful company and team in history.

THE DYNASTY FORMULA

The dynasty formula is simple: Dynasty = P4

Four building blocks—labeled P4—determine our success in business, the military, politics, religion, education, entertainment, sports, and many more areas. The four P's have also been the building blocks in the successes or failures of civilizations from the beginning of time.

Following is a short summary of this winning formula. It contains the four building blocks of who, what, how, and why. Without each of these blocks in place, a long-term dynasty status is not achievable. The formula gives a leader the best chance of developing a company, organization, or team that will not only be the best in class but will last long enough to be classified as a dynasty.

P1—PEOPLE—(WHO) This block focuses on the PEOPLE—the leaders at the top and their respective roles, interactions, and talents. This is the most important block to get right because it requires leaders with the specific traits needed to be successful.

P2—PERSONALITY TRAITS—(WHAT) It is not enough to have smart leaders in the perfect positions at the top. They have to have the essential PERSONALITY traits that will guide their decision-making behavior. Nine key traits were culled from hundreds of potential traits found in research and my experience with successful leaders. These traits (see page 49) are categorized under a C.H.A.R.A.C.T.E.R. paradigm that is easy to remember and utilize.

P3—PROCESS—(HOW) Even when the timing is good with smart leaders who display great character, failure can occur when the PROCESS is flawed. Selecting the wrong employees or an inability to plan, execute, or measure properly will keep an entity from sustaining itself over a long period of time.

P4—PURPOSE—(WHY) The foundation of these building blocks is PURPOSE. An intention to be the best in one's field of endeavor and the drive to achieve excellence may need no justification, but they do need an ethical core to prevent disasters like Madoff's. Purpose is spiritual and ethical business, comparable to business itself or determination to win, and it must prevade every aspect of a leader's life. Spectacular careers brought down by personal lapses in judgement, notably sexual, fill the tabloids every day. Given great power and exposure to public scrutiny, leaders serve as role models in the private sphere—willingly, knowingly, or not. Their public purpose fails with their ruined personal reputations, regardless of every other leadership skill in play.

Each of the four blocks is necessary to achieve that rare distinction of a dynasty. Flaws or weaknesses in one or more blocks explain why leaders fail. Use this model when evaluating a civilization, a country, a company, or any team challenged with the task of winning and beating the competition over a long period of time.

Each of these four blocks can be traced to its separate origin over the last eighty years in fields ranging from social (P1) and developmental psychology (P3) to clinical psychology (P2) and organizational psychology (P4).

THE CHAMPIONSHIP FORMULA		
P1—WHO?	**PEOPLE**	Thinker Promoter Coordinator
P2—WHAT?	**PERSONALITY**	C—Caring H—Honesty A—Attitude R—Resilience A—Analytical thinking C—Communication T—Teaching E—Energy R—Rules to live by
P3—HOW?	**PROCESS**	S—Select P—Plan E—Execute E—Educate D—Document
P4—WHY?	**PURPOSE**	Dream Love Mentor

This is the first time anyone has pulled these concepts together to produce a comprehensive formula that has proved to be accurate in explaining why these entities become winning dynasties.

LEADERSHIP AND WINNING

It is impossible to have a discussion on building a dynasty without a thorough understanding of leadership.

Leadership is a word used by many but truly understood by few. A thorough understanding of leadership is a prerequisite for developing a winning team.

We know that a great leader is essential for winning. But what do we know about leadership?

First, it is rare! Only the top 1 percent of all leaders are good, but the top one-tenth of 1 percent (one in a thousand) are great, based on research and confirmed by my experiences with top CEOs and legendary coaches.

Second, it's complex. If you were to conduct a meta-analysis (statistical analysis that summarizes numerous research studies on a given topic) and crunch all the data to come up with specific findings, you would walk away with the realization that much has been written but few firm conclusions can be drawn because of the complexity of leadership. The type of leader, the circumstances, and the era, are some variables to consider. Was the leader effective during his or her reign? Do others identify him or her as a role model?

WHAT DO WE REALLY KNOW ABOUT LEADERSHIP?

The study of leadership is greatly impacted by one's own viewpoint and the discipline from which leadership is studied. Listed below are some of the disciplines from which leaders have been studied.

- » History
- » Sports
- » Politics
- » Religion

» Business   » Finance

» Military   » Philosophy

» Psychology   » Anthropology

The psychological study of leadership is about one hundred years old, and amount of research conducted is enormous. Researchers at Kaplan DeVries reviewed ten meta-analysis studies to determine how leadership has been measured in past research. These analyses included evaluations of over 280,000 leaders from 1,124 samples and 1,695 statistical tests looking at the relationship of leader personality and effectiveness. The problem is that researchers define leadership in many ways. Mark Van Vugt and the coauthors of *Leadership, Fellowship, and Evolution* broadly define it in terms of (1) influencing individuals to contribute to group goals and (2) coordinating the pursuit of those goals. In practical terms, most view leadership as building a team and guiding it to a victory or a goal.

In short, the research on leadership, although extensive and sometimes broadly interpreted, provides us with useful generalizations about the links between personality, intellectual ability and leadership style and evaluations of leadership potential and performance (Bono and Judge T, 2004).

THE BEST LEADERS

It has been my passion to study the research on leadership these last thirty years. I have read hundreds of books covering thousands of companies and consulted with dozens of coaches at the pro and collegiate levels. The following people stand out as having contributed the most to my

BEST CEOs

Dozens of surveys of the best CEOs of all time identify the following individuals.

» AUTOMOTIVE

  * Henry Ford, Ford Motor Company

  * Alfred Sloan, General Motors Corporation

  * Lee Iacocca, Chrysler Corporation

» TECHNOLOGY

  * Steve Jobs, Apple

  * Andy Grove, Intel

  * Bill Gates, Microsoft

  * Lou Gerstner, IBM

» FINANCIAL

  * J.P. Morgan, J.P. Morgan & Co.

  * Warren Buffett, Berkshire Hathaway

  * Michael Bloomberg, Bloomberg, LP

» INDUSTRIAL

  * Andrew Carnegie, U.S. Steel

  * John D. Rockefeller, Standard Oil of New Jersey

» MEDIA

  * Katharine Graham, *Washington Post*

  * Oprah Winfrey, Harpo Productions

» RETAIL

  * Sam Walton, Wal-Mart Corporation

understanding of what it takes to be a leader of a championship company or coach of a championship team.

MANAGEMENT: Peter Drucker—the best mind on corporate leadership over the last sixty years. His influence in this country and in Japan has been enormous. He had an unbelievable impact on such current leaders as Jim Collins (*Good to Great*) and Reverend Rick Warren, pastor of Saddleback Church in Lake Forest, California, and author of *The Purpose Driven Life*. (See also *The Essential Drucker*, 2001).

CORPORATE LEADERS: Warren Bennis is by far the most respected writer on corporate leadership over the last thirty-five years, having studied and written about and talked to and consulted with the best Fortune 500 leaders in the world. (See all his books, especially *Why Leaders Can't Lead*, 1989).

MILITARY: Some of the most intriguing writings on military leaders are reported from Civil War works. The courage of Lincoln and the strategy of Generals and Grant (*Robert E. Lee on Leadership*, Crocker, H. W., 1999) are instructive.

The utilization of lessons learned in the military for businesses can also be found in the Marine Corps system (*Sempri Fi: Business Leadership the Marine Corps Way*, Carrison, D. and Walsh, R., 1999).

COACHING: My favorite books on sports leadership are by Tom Osborne (*More Than Winning*, 1985) and the legendary Mike Krzyzewski at Duke (*Successful Strategies for Basketball, Business, and Life*, 2000).

The best of all are eleven-time NBA championship coach Phil Jackson, (*More Than a Game*, 2001) whose philosophy on life and the psychology of coaching is unparalleled, and the very popular NFL coach Tony Dungy (*Quiet Strength*, 2007).

What all these leaders and their writings have in common, regardless of their time in history and their perspective, is their ability to capture the core essence of the type of leaders and the characteristics that led each of these individuals to be successful in their respective organization. Referring to Vince Lombardi's leadership, player Jerry Kramer said, "He made us all better than we thought we could be." That is the real essence of a dynasty leader!

Leaders today need knowledge. They are weary of theories, fables, and even success stories that, while interesting, don't apply to them. They need a more comprehensive blueprint to follow, one that they can plug into and measure against. I believe I have found a formula against which all entities can be measured, and which can be used in constructing a winning endeavor.

WHY ME?

I offer you an analysis of the top dynasties in business and sports for a clear understanding of how to achieve the dynasty distinction in your own work. Two running case studies involving Berkshire Hathaway and the University of Nebraska football team best illustrate the application of the P4 formula. These case studies are presented later in the text.

My credentials for presenting this P4 formula is predicated on the following:

» My experience as part of the staff of more than sixteen championship teams in multiple sports over the last three decades.

» My consulting to well over one hundred companies that have achieved remarkable success and are recognized as being among the best in the world.

» My long career of teaching and researching leadership and my findings on building and maintaining winning organizations.

» My review of more than three hundred top-selling books and articles that address these topics.

» My thorough analysis of the sociological and psychological research of how and why certain organizations have gone from good to great and dominated their respective fields for decades.

» My consulting with and mentoring of hundreds of CEOs and top executive leaders in corporations and more than fifty head coaches at the collegiate and pro levels all of whom have achieved at the very highest levels.

» My presentations to more than one thousand organizations and more than three hundred companies.

» My individual consultations to over ten thousand individuals in my clinical practice.

What I have come to understand is this: Losing is easy! Winning is hard. Very, very hard.

Losing can usually be traced to a lack of getting the right people in place, people with the essential personality traits who use the best processes for the right reasons.

Winning and continuing to win over a long period of time requires adherence to a formula, a set of building blocks essential to every successful endeavor.

Each of this volume's two sections will analyze this winning formula in more depth.

BUILDING A DYNASTY: PEOPLE & PERSONALITY

We attend motivational seminars, read books, receive extensive training, and work hard. But things simply don't change. Those who want to be better leaders are more discouraged than ever.

The United States Marine Corps has this excellent tagline: "The Few, The Proud, The Marines."

The meaning is that only a few people who are highly proud of their accomplishments can qualify to be a Marine.

And so it is with leaders in every organization since the beginning of time.

It starts at the top with the leaders and the personality traits that dictate the direction of an organization. This first section examines the three types of leaders at the top and their nine personality traits, six of which are covered in this section and three in the next. Each is critical to the success of their teams in the journey to become a dynasty.

Chapter 1

THE THREE TYPES
OF LEADERS

*Ability may get you to the top, but it takes character
to keep you there. —John Wooden*

I was excited but also apprehensive about my invitation. I had been invited to be interviewed before the entire football coaching staff at the University of Nebraska at Lincoln for a sports psychologist position with the football team.

It was a cold, dreary day in January of 1989—typical Nebraska weather.

For a small-town Nebraska native, the opportunity to work with Big Red was a dream. But my main motivation was to work with young people, to make a difference in their lives. I had to do something—because I was burning out!

I had one of the most—if not *the* most—successful and prestigious private practices in the state. I was head of the Medical Psychology Department in a large medical clinic. I was respected by the physicians and my patients. My psychotherapy load was heavy—fifty to sixty hours of therapy each week, plus phone calls, record keeping, paperwork, and meetings. I loved it! I was blessed with the opportunity to help a lot of people for a long time.

But it was intense. Some patients died. I got referrals from all medical specialties, from cancer to heart disorders to challenging chronic medical conditions. Addressing my patients' psychological needs was critical. Some of my patients experienced severe depression, difficult marriages, or workplace-behavior issues. Every one of my sixty patients each week deserved my best. And I had only one hour to help each person or couple.

For my own mental health, I had to get my mind off the worries. Practicing sports psychology was my outlet.

My interview with the coaches went well, thank goodness. I was surprised to hear soon after that they liked my competitive spirit. I did not realize that it had come through so clearly—I mean, I don't have to win at cards or golf, but if it's a team sport or individual competition, then I am wired!

I had just one meeting left to seal the deal. On my way down the hallway, it hit me. I was about to talk one on one with my longtime hero— head coach Tom Osborne. He was everything I wanted to be. He was voted high school athlete of the year in Nebraska and college athlete of the year. He played professional football, earned his Ph.D. in psychology from the same psychology department as I did. He even studied briefly at a seminary—as did I for four years.

This one-hour conversation changed my life.

Upon thoroughly checking my references, he hired me. His guidance on winning and losing taught me a great deal. I was very fortunate to work with the only head coach of a major sports team in the United States who held a Ph.D. in psychology. He specialized in statistics and research design—five times more difficult than my area. He just immediately understood what I wanted to do. Best of all he understood why, and I did not have to convince him of the things I wanted to do. He never formally talked about his psychological training—always humble—but a trained person could observe evidence of his psychological skills in how he related to others and in his extraordinarily, wise judgment. His strategic thinking was awe-inspiring to see in action. He could take a team apart on the sidelines and at half-time. General Patton would have loved him.

His humility and spirituality are perhaps what earned everyone's deepest respect. He is always steady and unflappable, but very, very competitive.

Tom Osborne is the perfect example of a dynastic leader. It is the people at the top—plus their personality traits, their processes, and their purpose in life—who provide a more complete answer to how companies and teams can reach dynasty status.

PI–PEOPLE

This part of the model identifies three core leadership staff members and a group of followers:

> » A *Thinker*—an idea person.
>
> » A *Promoter*—a marketer and communicator.
>
> » A *Coordinator*—a day-to-day manager.
>
> » A *Corps of Action-oriented Staff*—support staff.

WHO?
LEADERS AT
THE TOP

THINKER—The idea and knowledge person whose wisdom guides the organization.

PROMOTER—The person who represents the organization through his or her communication, marketing, and leadership skills.

COORDINATOR—The person who organizes and manages the organization.

LEADERSHIP STYLES

In their book *In Their Time*, Anthony Mayo and Nitin Nohria explain that researchers have identified three prototypical leadership styles:

- » The Entrepreneurial Leader
- » The Charismatic Leader
- » The Leader as Manager

My findings indicate that you need all three leadership styles at the top of an organization. Perhaps this is why so many leaders now last at the top for only three to five years. They don't surround themselves with the other styles. For example, we are in a period in which there are an abundance of charismatic leaders who lack deeper substance and who bounce from one rousing speech to the next. They are a mile wide and an inch deep. It can catch up to you during your first crisis.

If we match the Entrepreneur with the Thinker, the Charismatic with the Promoter, and the Manager with the Coordinator, you can see how all three styles are needed to run a successful organization. It is important to note that these three roles are all essential, whether they are formally labeled as CEO, COO, etc., or given informal names.

CHAMPIONSHIP FORMULA MODEL—WHO?

THINKER. This is the brains behind a team. He or she comes up with cutting-edge innovation that propels and maintains the group's success—Jobs with Apple or Tex Winter and the triangle offense with the Bulls and Lakers. They are brilliant people who can conceptualize and apply their vision with incredibly successful outcomes.

PROMOTER. This is the person who promotes, sells, or markets the team or company and the person the public most readily associates with it: Jack Welch, GE; Warren Buffett, Berkshire Hathaway; Peyton Manning, the Colts; or Jeff Gordon and Dale Earnhardt Jr., NASCAR.

COORDINATOR. This is the day-to-day coordinator who is responsible for running an organization. This is often the COO or the general manager of a team such as the brilliant GM of the Colts, Bill Polian.

ACTION-ORIENTED STAFF. These are the key chief executive officers, board members, division heads, assistant coaches, or administrative staffers who carry out daily functions that ensure the ongoing success of the organization.

INFLUENCER. This is a person who has had a major impact on the life of the key leader of a team—the person most identified as the primary leader. The Influencer impacts the culture, thinking, and behavior of the Leader whether he or she is in the role of Thinker, Promoter, or Coordinator. Influencers are mentors who may be a parent, coach, teacher, boss—anyone who helped shape the head coach or CEO.

The model is inherently embedded in all corporate and sports teams. Typically we see the following:

CHAMPIONSHIP TEAM MODEL: LEVELS		
Corporate	Board Chairman	*Thinker*
	CEO	*Promoter*
	COO	*Coordinator*
	Executive Team	*Action Staff*
Professional	Star Player	*Promoter*
	GM or Owner	*Coordinator*
	Head Coach	*Thinker*
	Assistant Coaches & Staff	*Action Staff*
College	Chancellor or President	*Coordinator*
	Athletic Director	*Promoter*
	Head Coach	*Thinker*
	Assistant Coaches & Staff	*Action Staff*

NOTE. These roles are not always locked in for all time. As brilliant thinkers build a large talent base at the top, they can then switch to promoting the organization—and become the face that people identify with as representing the organization. For example, Warren Buffett has been able to move into the Promoter role, with Charlie Munger and previously David

Sokol helping with the Thinker duties. So there needs to be great flexibility in this shifting, with contributions clearly spelled out for long-term success.

THE SHAPING OF A LEADER

John Wooden was impacted first by his father, Joshua, who lost their seventy-acre farm due to drought and tainted hog serum. He never whined or blamed others, and he taught his son to make no excuses. His advice to his son that John passed on to others: "Be true to yourself, help others, make each day your masterpiece, make friendship a fine art, drink deeply from good books—especially the Bible—build a shelter for a rainy day, give thanks for your blessings, and pray for guidance every day."

Wooden's school principal and coach, Earl Warriner, taught him a valuable lesson when Wooden left his game jersey at home when the team left for a road game. His coach would not let him borrow another one, and they lost an important game because John did not play. John learned that no one is more important than any other.

His chief mentor was Piggy Lambert, his Purdue head basketball coach. After three all-American seasons, Wooden was offered a lot of money to play pro ball before the NBA got started. He asked for Piggy's advice, and Piggy told him, "If you play in dirt you are bound to get dirty." So he followed his passion of teaching and went on to be the most successful collegiate coach of all time of all sports.

TEAM-TO-DYNASTY TIP #2. By studying the people who mentored and shaped a leader, you learn a great deal about the essence of a championship leader.

The influence and shaping of others by this winner of the Big Ten medal for scholarship and athletic prowess is displayed in the chart below.

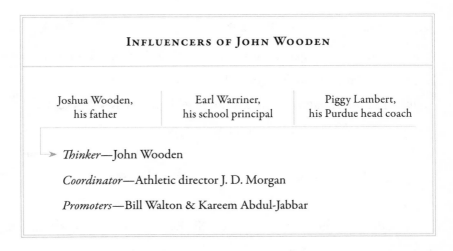

INFLUENCERS OF JOHN WOODEN		
Joshua Wooden, his father	Earl Warriner, his school principal	Piggy Lambert, his Purdue head coach

Thinker—John Wooden

Coordinator—Athletic director J. D. Morgan

Promoters—Bill Walton & Kareem Abdul-Jabbar

This model is fluid and is best understood in the context that the key person—CEO or head coach—may start out as the Thinker and later become the Promoter. They may even do all three jobs temporarily until a coordinator can be found. Clearly the roles of Thinker and Promoter are the most important. Also, understanding one's life-long mentors helps to understand the rout of a person's character. Wooden's athletic director, J. D. Morgan, came by one day to see him while he was working on his budget, travel, and planning duties. Morgan scooped up the entire stack of paperwork, threw it in a basket, and said, "John, you just coach and I will help with the rest." That's the essence of a great coordinator's role.

Bill Walton, Kareem Abdul-Jabbar, and dozens of all-stars and all-Americans became the faces of the UCLA program as they were very successful, albeit reluctantly at times, in their role of Promoter. Bill was rebellious—did not like control—and Kareem was shy and introverted. They went on to become two of the greatest players of all time. Their respect and love for their coach is remarkable. Almost all of John Wooden's players graduated, with a very high number of them receiving advanced degrees in medicine or law or playing pro ball for many years. His mentors and dream intact, Wooden was also fortunate enough to find his love, Nellie, his best friend and wife of fifty-three years.

DYNASTY & TEAMS

Within successful dynasties, there are many teams that contribute to its ongoing success.

CORPORATE TEAMS

DYNASTY: Berkshire Hathaway
> Buffett—*Promoter*
> Charlie Munger—*Thinker*
> CEOs of companies—*Coordinators*

TEAM: MidAmerican Energy (Berkshire Hathaway–controlled company)
> David Sokol, former chairman—*Thinker*
> Greg Abel, CEO—*Promoter*
> COOs of companies—*Coordinator*

SPORTS TEAMS

DYNASTY: Hendrick Motorsports
> Rick Hendrick, owner—*Promoter*
> Marshall Carlson, president and COO—*Coordinator*
> Jeff Andrews, engineer—*Thinker*

TEAM: Five-time NASCAR Championship Team #48

Jimmie Johnson, driver—*Promoter*

Chad Knaus, crew chief—*Thinker*

Ron Malec, car chief—*Coordinator*

THE CELTICS–THE GREAT DYNASTY

Simultaneous with the dynasty dominance of UCLA on college basketball during the late 1950s until the mid-1980s was the heyday of the Boston Celtics. They won eleven championships in thirteen years with eight in a row, the longest consecutive winning streak of any North American professional sports team between 1957 and 1969. They have won seventeen NBA championships—the most of any NBA franchise. Their decline from 1996 to 2007 was traced to the premature deaths of two star players—Len Bias and Reggie Lewis.

The team struggled early on in the franchise until it hired perhaps the greatest NBA coach of all time in Red Auerbach. He fulfilled the role of Thinker and put together his own "S.P.E.E.D. Process" with an unbelievable ability to recruit the best athletes. The first dynasty was made up of Bob Cousy and Bill Russell (five-time MVP), whom he acquired with some nifty behind-the-scene maneuvers. Bill Russell, who was voted one of the top-ten players of all time, turned out to be a tremendous Promoter for the franchise with his work ethic and leadership skills. Red's innovation of the fast break, much like Wooden's fast break and full-court press, revolutionized the game.

Auerbach's dynasties experienced some setbacks along the way when the role of Coordinator, played by various owners, went sour. The important lesson here is that even with the greatest coach in NBA history and play-ers like Russell, Parish, McHale and Bird, the franchise could not totally flourish without all three roles filled by great leaders. When they had that third role of coordinator filled with great owners, they really flourished.

The more recent building of the third Celtics dynasty occurred with the hiring of former player Danny Ainge, who has become the brilliant Thinker in trading for players like Kevin Garnett and Ray Allen. With Doc Rivers in the Coordinator role and Kevin Garnett as the Promoter, the team won the 2008 championship and nearly won the 2010 championship.

RED BULL RACING

Red Bull Racing has dominated the Formula One circuit. However, the easy success of the Red Bull Racing team in NASCAR can also be traced to the leadership at the top. While Red Bull Racing is relatively new to NASCAR, its numerous general managers have served as the Coordina-tors of the organization, while driver Brian Vickers of the #83 team has been the extraordinary Promoter for the team and has loved being the "edgy" PR campaigner for the product during the team's five-year run.

The Thinker of Red Bull Racing is the multibillionaire and founder of Red Bull—Dietrich Mateschitz. Voted the twenty-fifth most innova-tive and creative business person in the world, he founded and has guided his company to selling four billion cans of Red Bull a year (more than its next three energy-drink competitors, with $5 billion in annual revenue) by spending $300 million a year in marketing mostly on sports teams. It recently built a $225 million soccer stadium (Red Bull Stadium) in New York. Paid for in cash, it's the largest in North America.

THE NEBRASKA MODEL

The reason for Nebraska's unheard-of success in college football and for its place as the most dominating team in the 1990s was leadership team that launched this successful decade.

» Promoter: Bob Devaney was the successful head coach of football who turned a losing program around in the mid-1960s and became athletic director after turning the team over to Tom Osborne in 1973. Bob had an outgoing Irish personality, and everyone loved to be around him. He supported all of Tom's efforts, and everyone rallied around him.

» Thinker: Tom received his Ph.D. in psychology at Nebraska, specializing in statistical design and research. Only the brightest go into this field. He turned down a promising academic career— thank goodness. He loved to design plays, and no one could equal his sideline and halftime adjustments. Absolutely brilliant thinker! His power game and innovative style, and most important, the ability to motivate his entire staff and develop players, stand out. His resilient personality was exhibited in a remarkable record of at least nine wins a year for twenty-five straight years, unmatched by any modern-day coach.

» Coordinator: The brilliant chancellor of UN-Lincoln was Woody Varner. Tom's mentor and great friend was by far the best chancellor in the school's history. Supporting the program was a core action group of athletic staff and coaches, such as George Sullivan, head athletic trainer, and Ursula Walsh, director of academic support, plus many others.

» Influencer: The person or persons who most shaped and influenced the Promoter role through their mentorship, thereby influencing the behavior of the organization.

» Action Staff: This is the action-oriented group of individuals who carry out the mission of the leaders at the top (i.e., VPs, executive team members, assistant coaches, etc.).

LEADERS OF THE GREATEST WINNING DYNASTY

» Socrates—*Thinker*

» Plato—*Coordinator*

» Aristotle—*Promoter*

These ancient Greek philosophers and leaders emphasized the importance of seeking the truth. They were absolutely the most influential philosophers of all time, and certainly the leaders of the greatest dynasty ever, and they represent the three types of leadership roles (P1) that are critical to every single successful organization. If the ancient Greeks were building cars, Socrates, the Thinker, would have designed the car; Plato, the Coordinator, would have built it; and Aristotle, the Promoter, would have driven it around Athens for everyone's appreciation. Each role and each leader can be found in every single successful dynasty that lasts for a decade or more.

Chapter 2

THE CHARACTER OF A
DYNASTIC LEADER

I've never seen anyone derailed from top leadership because of a lack of
business literacy or conceptual skills; it's ALWAYS because of lapses in
judgment and questions about character. ALWAYS. —*Warren Bennis*

I hate to lose more than I love to win.

And I really, really love to win!

I clearly remember the exact moment this realization about myself
hit me; it was an epiphany. It happened on a dark rainy night in Charlotte, North Carolina. I was to meet with Dom Capers, the head coach of
the Carolina Panthers, at their stadium complex. (Dom later became the
defensive coordinator of Super Bowl champions the Green Bay Packers in
2011.)

As I walked into the coaches' meeting room, I recognized my good friend
Kevin Steele—the linebackers coach. All the other assistants were sitting
around a large table. I heard a loud voice from the defensive coordinator:
"Sixty and three? How the hell did you do it?" I turned around to see who he

was talking to and then it dawned on me. I was momentarily stunned. He was talking to me about our football team's record over the previous five years at Nebraska, where I was the team performance psychologist. The coordinator, highly respected, had just given me a tremendous compliment. We had just won three national college football championships in four years.

Sixty wins and three losses! Wow.

Three plays! Three lousy plays cost us the three games that would have really put us in the record books. As it was, we were the most dominant sports team in the 1990s at all levels and in all sports. Our 1995 team was voted not only the best college football team of all time, but the tenth-best sports team of all time—at any level.

The timing of my visit was ironic. I talked one-on-one with Coach Capers later that evening about his team's struggles. That very morning his starting quarterback, his promotional leader, was struggling and requested to be demoted, a very rare request. The quarterback left a five-year, $25 million contract on the table. It threw the entire organization into disarray. Capers eventually lost his job; the quarterback was traded following in-patient treatment. This experience reinforced my belief in how hard it is to win without the three types of leaders at the top.

My mantra is "One player, one play, one game can win or lose an entire season or championship." One person, one transaction, one day can bankrupt a large multibillion-dollar company.

I can't remember more than ten of the sixty wins during that streak, but I can remember every single play that lost us the three games. In NASCAR we have won and lost national championships by one-tenth of a second in one of the races or by one-tenth of a percent over a thirty-six-race season.

And so it is with all of us. *Everyone* wants to win! But winning is difficult. This level of difficulty seems to be growing as the speed and complexity of the competition continue to grow each year. We all want to be appreciated, respected, and happy. Or as the psychologist Abraham Maslow found, we want to reach our highest level of satisfaction—self-fulfillment!

In practical terms, it means we want to win in all areas of our lives.

Most importantly, the specific answers to *who, what, how,* and—most importantly—*why* are elusive. People want answers. The levels of dissatisfaction, discontent, and depression in our country are at an all-time high. From 9/11 in 2001 to the financial meltdown in 2008, we have clearly witnessed a decade with more failures than wins. We experienced the biggest bankruptcies in U.S. history in Bear Stearns, Lehman Brothers, and Enron—companies that everyone once touted as the best in the world in their respective fields for decades.

USC professor Warren Bennis has consulted with more CEOs than any other nationally recognized expert on leadership. He is particularly knowledgeable about leadership failures (see the quotation that opens this chapter), as I have observed dozens of times in working with leaders at the top. As Bennis points out, leaders who fail do so primarily because of flaws in their character. If we have learned anything from corporate failures and the demises of once-proud sports franchises such as the Detroit Lions of the NFL, we can clearly see in retrospect the numerous character flaws behind these once unimaginable failures of organizations that have dominated their industry for many decades.

WHY LEADERS FAIL

In the beginning we have so much hope for our leaders and where they will take us in the future that we often ignore the present and the signs that lead to their failure.

A few years ago I attended and presented to the American Football Coaches Association at their annual conference. They presented the Coach of the Year award to Mark Mangino, who they saw as a hero for turning around the Kansas football program. Two years later he was fired for alleged abuse of players.

Temple University psychologist Frank Farley coined the term *Type-T Personality*, which describes the kind of personality that is drawn to careers that require a willingness to step out of ordinary life and take risks (the *T* stands for *thrill seeker*). You have to be a risk taker to establish a winning dynasty. But if you don't have each of the four "P" factors described in this book to guide you, particularly the C.H.A.R.A.C.T.E.R. personality traits, you will fail.

Handling high-pressure, challenging tasks can become addictive. For some high-profile leaders, that level of pressure, in combination with opportunities to behave unethically, has led to failure. We can learn from their unethical behavior.

My experience (thousands of interviews, interventions, and therapy) allowed me to have insights into deceitful, unethical leaders and uncover the top ten reasons why leaders fail. The reasons are not in any priority ranking, and often multiple reasons contribute to a leader's demise.

TOP TEN REASONS LEADERS FAIL	
Greed	"I'm going to get mine since everyone else is. And besides, I deserve it. Look at what I have done."
Insecurity	"I can't count on anyone and I hope my inadequacies are not discovered."
Power	"I am in control—I want and get the attention I need."
Arrogance	"I am better than anyone else."
Narcissism	"I am the best and most important and only my needs count."
Paranoia	"I never trust anyone—there's no such thing as loyalty."
Manic behavior	"I am obsessively driven—which gives me energy to succeed."
Addictions	"I need drugs, alcohol, gambling, and sexual gratification to get by."
Burnout and depression	"I hide my depression, but it is a subconscious reason for my irrational behavior."
Inability to love	"Nobody ever loved me, so why should I care about others?"

THE BASIS OF FAILURE:
LACK OF MORAL DEVELOPMENT

In all the companies I consult with and among the hundreds of CEOs, coaches, and leaders I provide counsel to, I find that the number-one predictor of success is their level of moral development. Personal happiness today is often determined not by how much you make, the company you work for, or even what you do—it's directly impacted by who your boss is and his or her level of moral development.

What causes these "fatal flaws" in the personality of our leaders? I always had a hard time figuring out why these seemingly bright, talented, well-educated leaders could fail so spectacularly, and often so abruptly. Then I remembered my training on moral development.

Developmental psychologist Lawrence Kohlberg developed a theory of moral development based on stages that a person progresses through. If you don't pass through each stage during your childhood, you will become "stuck" in the highest stage you attain, and that stage will govern your moral behavior. In my opinion this perhaps explains at least some of the reasons why leaders fail.

STAGES OF MORAL DEVELOPMENT—
WHY DOESN'T EVERYBODY DO THE RIGHT THING?

STAGE 1 Avoiding punishment (the most basic stage of moral development, often found in young children).

STAGE 2 Serving self-interest (a dangerous stage to be stuck in morally, where the focus is "What's in it for me?" and where moral decisions are based on "What can I get out of it?").

STAGE 3 Seeking approval from others (the stage usually occurs during one's teens, when one behaves in a way that he or she thinks will live up to the expectations of others).

STAGE 4 Following authority (someone in this stage does as told and follows the rules).

STAGE 5 Respect for social order (in this stage of moral development, one's behavior is driven by the desire to maintain social order and avoid chaos in society).

STAGE 6 Universal ethical principles (in this highest stage of moral development, one is guided by conscience and universal moral principles).

The followers of leaders—be they employees, colleagues, fans, members of a religious group, or the rank and file of a military branch—want and need their leaders and heroes and to have character that is infused with the highest level of moral development. We want to follow and believe in someone whose personality traits we admire. It's the glue that keeps us united.

TEAM-TO-DYNASTY TIP #3. Be aware of the stage of moral development of both yourself and of those leaders you choose to follow.

There is one question I constantly hear today: "Where are all the men and women of character?" Obviously, people's behavior is more transparent today. There is less privacy and ability to get by with things than in the past decades and centuries. Leaders in the public realm can no longer hide character deficits. There is very little privacy, and a flaw in moral character is often exposed in the media, typically in an embarrassing manner.

TEAM-TO-DYNASTY TIP #4. You can easily judge the character of a person by the way he or she treats those who can do nothing for him or her.

The very best leaders I have been privileged to work with do a great deal to help others, and frequently nobody even knows about it.

Now we know that it's essential not only to have the right people in the right place, but to have the right people with the right personality traits to assure and sustain their success.

WHAT IS CHARACTER?

Popular books written by everybody from charismatic leaders and politicians to historical war leaders and championship coaches have offered their versions of what worked. Psychological research on leadership and teams covers personality traits, skills, behaviors, laws, habits, and principles—often with a number attached: The Seven Habits; 21 Laws; The Five Dysfunctions; The Four Obsessions; and so on. While all these contributions add to our body of knowledge, it comes to us in bits and pieces. I often find leaders simply want a method or formula that is summarized in such a way that they can remember it, follow it, and use it to improve their daily lives. If a specific formula is available to adapt to their situation, then they can carry it around in their minds and say, "Oh, yes. I can do these things to solve this challenge." The problem is that it is hard to take in all the parts of the formula and use it in a consistent way for daily success.

I have tried to summarize all the research and knowledge we have on leadership and apply it in a way that enables you to use these findings as core principles in guiding your daily decisions and behaviors. There are lots of adjectives one could list, and the number of personality traits could be in the hundreds. However, an in-depth analysis reveals that there are nine core traits that leaders must embody if they are to be truly successful. Each of these traits was carefully culled from a large database of research on very successful leaders over three thousand years of history and matched with my experience in consulting with and researching some of the most successful dynasties of all time. The best leaders will display all nine traits, but usually they are known especially for one trait in particular.

These nine personality traits are forged over time as one progresses through his or her respective stages of moral development. Deficits in one's moral development will result in the inability to fully develop these traits and will impede a leader's success.

P2—PERSONALITY

My patients have taught me a great deal about character. I saw enough hurt, pain, and tragedy to last many lifetimes.

It was difficult to let go at times—to not lose sleep.

I soon learned that those who made it revealed that they had a rock-solid character with outstanding personality traits, regardless of what life threw at them.

One patient, a very successful businessman, stands out in my memory. He grew up in a humble setting and went on to earn an MBA, eventually becoming the CEO of a very large Fortune 500 company. He made millions. In his first therapy session for marital problems, he bluntly asked how much money I made and commented on my rather cheap watch, as he was wearing an expensive Rolex. He was stuck in Stage 3 of his moral development, seeking approval from others. He displayed many of the reasons for his failure as a leader—greed, arrogance, paranoia, and mostly an inability to connect to others.

Our sessions worked—for a while. He could not keep it all together and eventually divorced and left town for bigger and better things. He was in the national press; he was hailed as a great leader. He died in his fifties, alienated from his kids and with few friends, lonely and far away from home.

TEAM-TO-DYNASTY TIP #5. "Character cannot be developed in ease and quiet. Only through experience of trial and suffering can the soul be strengthened, vision cleared, ambition inspired, and success achieved." —Helen Keller

---

Helen Keller was correct—it is always about character! Without character, you will eventually be exposed and fail.

WHAT?
CORE
PERSONALITY
TRAITS

CARING—Unconditional concern for others with genuine empathy.

HONESTY—Being open, candid, and transparent in establishing trust with all individuals, with a sense of humor and humility.

ATTITUDE—A positive perception of reality that guides our behavior and views of the world.

RESILIENCE—Our ability to rebound from life's setbacks no matter how difficult.

ANALYTICAL THINKING—The wisdom, vision, thinking, knowledge, and ability to guide others and make correct decisions.

COMMUNICATION—The ability to share one's thoughts, feelings, and decisions, in order to move others toward the desired direction.

TEACHING—The sharing, shaping, and improving of knowledge and behavior through instruction.

ENERGY—The hard work, passion, and mental toughness required to accomplish great things by and with others.

RULES TO LIVE BY—Rules for how to live your life guided by morals and ethics in all thoughts and behaviors.

The winning formula for taking an organization from a team to a dynasty requires the first step of identifying the people at the top who can perform the three roles—but that is not enough. Each of these three leaders must possess a core set of traits that are infused in all their behaviors—what we label their "personality."

The first six of these nine critical personality traits are covered in the next four chapters. Each trait—caring, honesty, attitude, resilience, analytical thinking, and communication—is covered more deeply and placed alongside case studies of best-in-class dynasties, from the corporate world and the world sports.

Chapter 3

DYNASTIC LEADERS ARE CARING & HONEST

Some people come into our lives and quickly go. Some stay for a while, leave footprints on our hearts, and we are never, ever the same. —Flavia Weedn

I don't remember her name, but I do remember her! She was a patient of mine who saw me for depression a number of years ago.

She left a footprint on my heart and changed my behavior.

When I asked her the cause of her depression, she explained that she was a divorced mother raising three young kids on her own. Her youngest daughter was disabled due to rubella and had significant vision and hearing loss.

There was no local school program available to provide unique services to the deaf and blind kids in the area. So she would get up at 5:00 a.m. each morning and drive one hour to take her daughter to school, then return home, take her other kids to school, and work all day. She would then drive again to pick her daughter up and bring her home, as there were no residential services available.

As she told me her story, I sat back and just looked at her in disbelief. A single mom driving four hours a day, working full-time, and taking care of her three kids. Amazing!

She was my hero.

Through all the years of working with wealthy, famous, brilliant, and/or popular people, I learned from this woman that the single most important personality trait, at least to start with, was an ability to love, to care for others.

Not only is it a powerful asset for a leader; love is also essential to being truly happy in life.

This experiential belief was reinforced in a recent anniversary trip I made to Prague—a beautiful city spared from the bombings of WWII.

We were having dinner and were joined by a young couple from Russia. I could tell the woman was madly in love with her shy boyfriend. So I prodded him to ask her to marry him, saying she was special.

She looked at me and said, "Why do you say that?" I responded, "Because you have a deep capacity to love." (Such observational skills I learned in reading people through thousands of therapy hours.)

She looked at me and said, "That's the nicest thing anyone has ever said about me." As I thought about it, it became clear to me that that's the nicest thing anyone could say about any one of us!

CARING—to be fond of, to like, to have concern for; guardianship or protection. Caring is essential for all human existence.

HONEST—to not lie; to be upright, frank, open, and to obtain things by fair means.

When people accept a leader, whether of a small team or a whole nation, they are saying, in effect, "Care about me and my interests. Be honest with me about things that affect my interests." A leader who does that will have their loyalty, and one who doesn't, won't. A trustworthy leader enables people to believe that he or she has security and predictability in life. People's belief in security and predictability also makes civilization possible. But all that a leader can guarantee is that the people he or she leads are heard and cared for and that he or she's telling them the truth.

TEAM-TO-DYNASTY TIP #6. The guiding principle in our quest for happiness is our instinct for self-preservation, which concerns our ability to be secure and to predict that this security will continue.

The Better Business Bureau is a consumer's guide to how trustworthy businesses are, and it serves a useful function in ranking companies on their business ethics. Its logo is "Start with trust." I also recently observed a business equipment company's cars with the words "Honesty is at the core of everything we do" painted on their bumpers. These companies have identified the one key personality trait they want people to associate with them.

Leadership findings and my own experience as a psychotherapist indicate that if you just care about others and are honest with them, they will cut you a great deal of slack because they know where your heart is and that your intentions are altruistic.

A number of my former patients have forever changed my life by sharing the important virtues of caring and honesty. A few cases stick out most in my mind.

Joe. While he was a college student Joe was severely burned in an apartment fire. He was dependent on a ventilator for breathing and was bedridden. Following his injuries he lived with his parents and had few visitors. His biggest fear was that electrical power would fail along with his backup batteries and he would not be able to breathe. I tried to give him some small amount of happiness during my many visits. I benefited from our visits perhaps far more than he did.

Mary Jane. She was a single mom who had raised her only child, a son, by herself since he was two years old. She came home from work one day and found him dead from a self-inflicted gunshot wound. She was devastated.

Carla. She wanted to know what to tell her young son, age three, where his father was. Her husband had been killed in an automobile accident the week before and her own father—"papa" to her son—was in a coma.

Emily. The young twenty-eight-year-old mother of three kids was just diagnosed with terminal cancer. She wanted to know what and how to tell her children that her time with them would be less than a year.

Carrie. A young twenty-six-year-old woman was on vacation with her fiancé when road conditions became treacherous. She asked her fiancé to drive, and only miles later the car turned over and instantly killed him. She put a rose on his grave every day for an entire year. She did not want to go on. I tried to give her a purpose in life.

I could write about many more. I never get the visions of these patients' faces out of my mind.

No one trained me for these situations. You get the basic principles, but it also depends a great deal on the therapist's own personality and ability to connect.

I was not always quite sure how to best help them, as there is no exact script to follow or science to guide me. I found that giving them my home

phone number, the option to call twenty-four hours a day, and deep sup-
portive caring made all the difference in their adjustment. In a world that
has become increasingly self-centered, people most of all just want to
know that you care about them and that you will be there for them when
they need someone, and that you will be honest with them. This allows
them to have security and predictability, which are powerful psychological needs for us all.

TOM OSBORNE AND THE NEBRASKA DYNASTY

Tom Osborne is one of the most caring and compassionate people I have
ever known. One of the great blessings in my life has been the opportunity
to work with him for the last twenty years. He is by far the most respected
and admired person in Nebraska. I grew up in the same town, attended a
seminary like him, and received my Ph.D. in the same psychology department. Tom Osborne was always the person I looked up to most. High
school and college athlete of the year, pro player, and then head coach, he
is now athletic director at Nebraska.

Less than 1 percent of the population is like Dr. Tom, in that he can
touch your mind and your heart, and most important, reach in and grab
hold of your soul. His thousands of players love him like a father.

An early-fall football game against a very good Arizona State football
team at home in 1995 best depicts this reciprocal love between Tom and
his players. A star player had gotten in trouble the previous week. When
Osborne benched him for the rest of the season, he was nationally criticized for not kicking the player off the team. The press reported it as a bru-
tal beating. Never happened that way. If the real truth had been known,

people's opinion might have totally changed. What Osborne would not tell people, even to this day, is that he kept this young man on the team and let him play in the bowl game because he was concerned about what he would do to himself. It worked for a while, as the structure of the program, the only support system this player had, kept him focused. Once away from the program, he fell apart. He was considered the number-one pick in the NFL draft. But Tom got him treatment and supported him. Many top head coaches told me point blank that they would not put their job on the line like that for any player. But Tom always puts others ahead of himself.

During the '95 championship season, it was just the players and me in the locker room before the Arizona State game for our team prayer and our psych-up session.

The team leader—a 310-pounder who was the toughest player I ever met—with tears in his eyes said, "This man is like my father, and nobody criticizes my father in our house." The score at halftime was 63–10. The final score was 77–28. Tom tried to hold it down in the second half by not passing, substituting, and running basic plays. It was the most points ever scored by halftime in Nebraska's history. The team was very fired up over the man they loved so much—they could have beaten anyone that day.

TEAM-TO-DYNASTY TIP #7. The person at the top will determine the personality or culture of an entire civilization, country, company, or team.

If you have a caring person at the top, exhibiting this behavior on a consistent basis, the culture takes on his or her personality. John Kotter at

Harvard (*What Leaders Really Do*, 1999) and Ed Schein at MIT (*The Corporate Culture Survival Guide,* 1999) are the two giants in this field. Their research backs up the incredible impact one person can have on the rest of the organization. These rare and exceptional leaders that make up less than 1 percent of the population can inspire a nation, make billions for a corporation, or win championships for a team at all levels.

THE CARING TRAIT OF TOM OSBORNE: ESSENCE OF A DYNASTY LEADER

From the twenty-plus years I had the privilege of working with Tom Osborne, I have some remarkable observations.

He never used swear words! He never disrespected or embarrassed anyone. He never screamed, yelled, or put anyone down! He was compassionate and displayed a caring pat on the shoulder to his players. He established and funded, along with his wife, Nancy, the "TeamMates" program—a mentoring program for at-risk youth.

He enjoyed daily scripture reading and meditation and opened every meeting with a prayer.

He donated all proceeds from his five books to charity and all camp money back to his assistant coaches.

He made hospital visits and phone calls and wrote letters of recommendation for over a thousand individuals during his career.

He donated vast amounts of time to the Fellowship of Christian Athletes.

He is one of the finest individuals I have ever met in my life.

ACCOMPLISHMENTS

In his twenty-five years of coaching Tom had a 255–49–3 record. His ten-plus wins per season average with a 83.6 percent, the fifth-best winning percentage of all time.

His most remarkable record, however, is that he always won at least nine games each year for his entire twenty-five-year career as head coach.

He is a former U.S. congressman and a College Football Hall of Fame coach.

He was a National Coach of the Year and an eight-time Conference Coach of the Year.

He was the all-time Conference Coach and Coach of the Decade (1990s).

His 1990s decade record is 108–16–1, three national championships in 1994, 1995, and 1997, and a 60–3 record during the last 5 years of his career.

TEAM-TO-DYNASTY TIP #8. "The first and last thing required of genius is the love of truth." —Goethe

A PSYCHOLOGICAL PORTRAIT OF WARREN BUFFETT

If you could have lunch or dinner with one person in the world, who would you choose? Would it be a president, a prime minister, a religious leader, a sports superstar, or a Nobel Prize winner?

I would like to do all of the above.

Having said that, I have a hard time imagining a better experience than having had dinner with the wealthiest man in the world. Yes, I was fortunate enough to have this experience, thanks to Warren Buffett's colleague David Sokol—one of my valued friends! Each year for the past ten years, an individual in the financial sector will bid as high as $2.6 million at the annual auction to do just that—have dinner with Warren Buffett. Buffett donates the money to charity. Having paid nothing but having been invited to sit with Warren, the first thing to hit me was how down-to-earth and personable he was. "Hi. I'm Warren Buffett," he said as he extended his hand for a friendly shake. In talking with Warren, I mentioned that I worked as the performance psychologist with his beloved Nebraska football team—the college he had graduated from. His wife, Astrid, said Warren could use my help with his bridge game. He explained that it is sometimes difficult to fall asleep at night as he sees bridge hands and his mind is so active. So I sent him one of my relaxation CDs—a cost to me of about $3. He sent me a full-page personal thank-you note for my gesture. Amazing! Insightful!

As a resident of Omaha, I have been fortunate to attend Berkshire Hathaway shareholder meetings. I have also been fortunate to observe Warren in numerous settings in addition to the shareholder meetings—at numerous fundraising events where he entertained in a skit or shared his wisdom, or at community events and interviews ranging from those with his buddy Bill Gates to various dignitaries. What emerges is a picture of a man who is amazingly at peace with himself, happy, humorous, humble, compassionate, and most of all honest. He is obviously brilliant—but in a unique way. His single greatest trait is perhaps his ability to take complex and difficult information and reduce it to a basic level that everyone can understand. This is the psychological essence of Warren Buffett—a person who works in a complex, sophisticated world and simplifies his life. That speaks eloquently as to why he is the leader of the most successful financial dynasty of the past hundred years. His behavior is in direct contrast to the sometimes headline-seeking behavior of his peers at this level.

BUFFETT = HONESTY & HUMILITY

National headlines and rankings of the person most often sought after by the media on honesty issues is Warren Buffett. From President Obama to the mainstream media, Buffett is the most frequently quoted person. It is not an accident. For his candid honesty, he is trusted by almost everyone, regardless of their political or philosophical views.

THE GREATEST FINANCIAL DYNASTY OF THE TWENTIETH AND TWENTY-FIRST CENTURIES

Warren Buffett was selected as the most admired corporate director in America by his peers—directors of boards and CEOs. National surveys identify him as the most trusted corporate leader in America. He is admired for both who he is, how he has conducted himself, and what he has accomplished for his shareholders.

If only my parents had invested $10,000 in him when I graduated from high school! Since our house back then was worth less than $10,000, it would have been a stretch, but we would be worth $20 million today if it had been invested with Buffett. Buffett has averaged more than 20 percent returns each year for over forty-five years, and no one else comes even close. Only two other funds were even remotely close according to the

Wall Street Journal. Fidelity's Magellan Fund averaged 16.3 percent and would be worth $9 million today, and the Templeton Growth Fund at 13.4 percent would be worth $3 million for comparison, while the S&P 500 averaged 9.3 percent or would be worth $560,000 today—big difference. Today, the spreads between these funds and Berkshire Hathaway grow ever greater.

Warren Buffett started buying Berkshire Hathaway shares in 1962 and took control of the company in 1965. The shares at the time he took over were worth around $15. As the chart below illustrates, the stock briefly hit $150,000 on December 11, 2007. It was what Peter Lynch has labeled a "10,000 bagger," an extremely rare phenomenon.

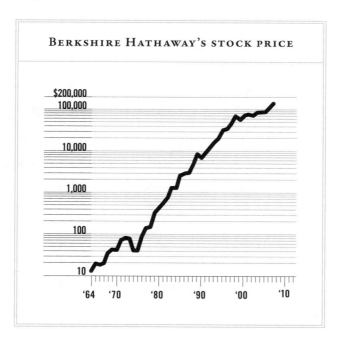

Warren Buffett is the leader in the world today who most epitomizes the leadership trait of honesty. Mr. Buffett could have also been listed as the best representative of many traits—analytical thinking, etc. However, integrity, honesty, teaching, and trust have always been more important than any other trait to him and to the people he associates with. Perhaps that is why he is one of the three wealthiest people in the world today.

Buffet and his good friend Bill Gates are both giving away their entire wealth to the Bill and Melinda Gates Foundation. Together they have also encouraged the top five hundred billionaires to commit half their wealth to charity.

Often associated with the trait of honesty are the co-traits of humility and humor. Mahatma Gandhi was a world leader whose dry sense of humor and a burning desire for seeking the truth changed an entire country for centuries. That is how powerful these personality traits can be in the hands of a winning leader.

Warren Buffett is well known for his sense of humor, often poking fun at himself. His annual reports and frequent TV appearances reveal this side of him. When commenting on the economy in February 2008 when the markets "tanked," he warned, "You only learn who has been swimming naked when the tide goes out." In 2009, when commenting on how long it would take to resolve the complex economic issues, he stated, "You can't produce a baby in one month by getting nine women pregnant."

TEAM-TO-DYNASTY TIP #9. "A sense of humor can help you overlook the unattractive, tolerate the unpleasant, cope with the unexpected, and smile through the unbearable." —Moshe Waldoks

Once a leader establishes his credibility by demonstrating that he cares about and is honest with those who follow him, he is then able to apply additional personality traits that can take his team to unimaginable accomplishments.

Chapter 4

ATTITUDE AND RESILIENCE
IN DYNASTIC LEADERS

The longer I live, the more I realize the impact of attitude on life . . .
The only thing we can do is play on the one string we have, and that
is our attitude. I am convinced that life is ten percent what happens
to me and ninety percent how I react to it. And so it is with you.
We are in charge of our attitudes. —*Charles Swindoll*

Bad attitude! How many times have we heard that description of someone? Usually they are cynical, negative, complaining people whom we all want to avoid being around.

We are attracted to people who smile, give us energy, are upbeat, and have that positive attitude no matter how bad things get.

Perhaps the greatest leader I have ever known had a very special attitude. As an infant he contracted meningitis and was severely disabled by the brain inflammation and subsequent damage. He had significant difficulty with vision and hearing, was essentially paralyzed, and was tube-fed. He was on a great deal of medication, had daily seizures, and endured unbelievable pain over twenty surgeries and fifty hospitalizations. He required twenty-four-hour care.

He never spoke a word—but his eyes said it all. He would beam whenever his close caregivers or family were with him. He never showed a bad or ungrateful attitude during his entire life of nearly thirty one years.

Every person who ever came in contact with him remarked on how he changed their lives. Many have dedicated their lives to serving others as a result of being with him. We are much better people for having known him and his inspiring attitude. John was a very special son.

ATTITUDE IS EVERYTHING

It turns out that there is a great deal of unhappiness in the world, with depression rates rising despite our ever-increasing standards of living. In the next twenty years, depression will replace cancer and heart disease as the number-one health problem in the world, according to the World Health Organization. What in the name of Freud is going on?

Perhaps our attitude plays a major role in how we perceive reality and react to it. We often look at what we don't have instead of how good we have it despite the challenges and obstacles.

All great leaders, even those with impressive accomplishments under their belts, have to have a winning attitude to be successful. As Vince Lombardi said, "Winning is not everything, but making the effort to win is." That's what a winning attitude is—being the best you can possibly be. (Maraniss 1999)

To best illustrate the application of this personality trait, I have selected three of the greatest dynasties in the sport of basketball: one at UCLA under Coach John Wooden (who passed away in 2011) and two NBA teams under Phil Jackson (who retired this year). Each story provides unique insight into the role that attitude played in the lives of these successful leaders.

THE UCLA DYNASTY

"There has never been a finer coach in American sports than John Wooden, or a finer man," said Rick Reilly in *Sports Illustrated* (2000). Recognized by many as one of the three greatest coaches of all time, along with Vince Lombardi and Knute Rockne, Wooden made a record that will never be matched—ever. He won seven national championships in a row (four in a row is the next best, and that is rare) and ten championships in twelve years and went on with an eighty-eight-game undefeated streak. Wooden, nicknamed the "Wizard of Westwood," was not only the most successful in terms of winning, but was perhaps the most admired coach ever because of his attitude.

Over twenty-seven years he won 620 games with never a losing season, but his legacy extends beyond that. He had only three rules. No profanity. No tardiness. No criticizing fellow teammates. "What you are as a person is far more important than what you are as a basketball player," was his chief message.

In 2009, Wooden was named the greatest coach of all time by 118 Hall of Famers, championship coaches, and sports experts as reported in *Sporting News* magazine. ESPN name Wooden the greatest coach of the twentieth century. We may never see someone of his accomplishments again.

His book *My Personal Best: Life Lessons from an All-American Journey* (2004) recounts his personal philosophy, forged by his humble, formative beginnings and his all-American years in Indiana High School and Purdue University. He was a great teacher, caring, humble, and honest. All of the nine personality traits in this book were epitomized by him, illustrating perhaps that his success was no fluke but the result of his leadership skills. One of my favorite quotations I share with leaders in business and sports is from John Wooden: "Be more concerned with your character than with your reputation, because your character is what you really are, while your reputation is merely what others think you are."

TEAM-TO-DYNASTY TIP #10. Be more concerned with your character than with your reputation, because character is what you really are. People will question you or criticize you, and there will be times you may even doubt yourself. But if you take care of your character and maintain a positive attitude through the tough times, your dynasty will prevail.

THE PYRAMID MODEL

Wooden's attitude toward life and basketball is best embodied in his "Pyramid of Success." Formulated more than fifty years ago, it is amazing to see how influential this model has become for all sports at all levels, as well as in corporate America.

The pyramid contains fifteen blocks ranging from Loyalty to Confidence and has ten unifying principles tying the blocks together, ranging from Integrity to Honesty (sounds similar to the nine characteristics of C.H.A.R.A.C.T.E.R.), which Wooden felt was the prime characteristic of a true team player.

TEAM-TO-DYNASTY TIP #11. "Success is peace of mind, which is a direct result of self-satisfaction in knowing you made the effort to do the best of which you are capable." —John Wooden

THE BULLS & LAKERS DYNASTIES

Phil Jackson, the former Chicago Bulls coach and former Lakers coach, has topped Red Auerbach with the most NBA championships—eleven. Only five coaches have won more than two titles—Pat Riley, five, and Gregg Popovich, four. He won eleven of the past twenty championships and has won 71 percent of games in the regular season and 70 percent in playoffs. He has twice as many victories in the post-season list as the next coach. Prestigious national panels selected Wooden as number one and Phil Jackson number four on the list of the best coaches of all time.

This focus on attitude in sports, business, and life is best addressed by Phil Jackson in his book *Sacred Hoops: Spiritual Lessons of a Hardwood Warrior*. This is one of my all-time favorite books. It gives great insight into how this Zen master has achieved something so remarkable in all of sports: winning eleven national championships with two different franchises—Bulls and Lakers—with three different superstars, Michael Jordan, Kobe, and Shaq.

His philosophy and emphasis on attitude is shaped, as he discusses in his book, by a mixture of traditional Christianity (his parents were missionaries), Zen Buddhism (he practices), and Lakota Sioux practices (from his experience on the reservation growing up in Fargo, North Dakota). Phil, better than anyone, could take superstars and change their attitudes. He could make them better team players by going to the next level using techniques of mindfulness, a focusing/concentration process, and by his ability to treat each player individually and differently based on each one's personality, while at the same time treating everyone equally—not an easy task. He would assign books to individual players and constantly challenge them to be selfless and compassionate. Here's the winning formula of the Jackson teams:

> » *Influencers*—Red Holzman (of the Knicks)
> Bill Fitch (of the University of North Dakota and the Celtics)

> » *Thinker*—Phil Jackson.

> » *Promoters*—Michael Jordan (six-time MVP and national championship)
> Kobe Bryant
> Shaq O'Neil

> » *Coordinators*—Tex Winter (inventor of the triangle offense)
> Jerry Krause (Bulls general manager)
> Jerry West (Lakers general manager)

Did these three superstars make Phil Jackson or did he make them? Perhaps they made each other, pushing each other to a higher level of performance. Along the way, he helped make the Lakers second in NBA net worth at $560 million and the Bulls third at $500 million (*Forbes*, December 2008).

TEAM-TO-DYNASTY TIP #12. "Winning is an attitude . . . and the attitude of the leader of the pack usually determines the speed of the pack!" —Phil Jackson.

THE ATTITUDE OF WARREN BUFFETT

In 1983, at the time of the Blue Chip Stamps merger with Berkshire Hathaway, Warren Buffett set down thirteen owner-related business principles that he thought would help new shareholders understand his managerial approach: he "eats his own cooking." As he states, 99 percent of his net worth is in Berkshire and 90 percent of Charlie Munger's family's net worth is also in Berkshire. Warren usually says something like this at his annual shareholder meeting in Omaha: "Charlie and I cannot promise you results. But we can guarantee that your financial fortunes will move in lockstep with ours for whatever period of time you elect to be our partner. We have no interest in large salaries or options or other means of gaining an edge over you. We want to make money only when our partners do and in exactly the same proportion. Moreover, when I do something dumb, I want you to be able to derive some solace from the fact that my financial suffering is proportional to yours . . . We believe candor benefits us as managers. The CEO who misleads others in public may eventually mislead himself in private." (2008 Berkshire Hathaway annual report, pp. 90–92).

BERKSHIRE HATHAWAY LEADERSHIP MODEL

Influencers—

Columbia Business School teachers Benjamin Graham & David Dodd	Ernest (grandfather) grocery store owner Howard (father) congressman & stockbroker

> *Promoter*—Warren Buffett

Thinker—Charlie Munger and Warren Buffett

Coordinator—CEOs of all companies owned or invested in

RESILIENCE

Resilience is another crucial factor in building a team into a dynasty. With the proper attitude and resilience, a team can overcome all adversities to evolve into a dynasty.

Abraham Lincoln was born in 1809, and his infant brother died in 1812. Six years later, when Abe was nine, his mother died. In 1928, his married sister died during childbirth. Abe failed in business at age twenty two and was defeated when he ran for state legislator in 1832. He tried another business in 1833. It failed. His fiancée, Ann Rutledge, died in 1835. He had a nervous breakdown in 1836. In 1843 he ran for Congress and was defeated. He tried again in 1848 and was defeated again. In 1850, his second son, three-year-old Edward, died. He tried running for the Senate in 1855. He lost. The next year he ran for vice president and lost. In 1859 he ran for the Senate again and was defeated. In 1860, the man who signed his name "A. Lincoln" was elected the sixteenth president of the United States. In 1862, the president's third son, Willie, died at age eleven. The president's wife, Mary Todd Lincoln, was emotionally devastated and never fully recovered.

Historians are split on whether George Washington or Abe Lincoln was our greatest president. Yet reviewing the obstacles he overcame and the resilience of his personality, we can clearly understand how Lincoln united this country in its development as a true dynasty.

Why select resilience as one of the nine critical characteristics of leadership? Because on earth there is pain and suffering, and it is how we deal with it that sets us apart. Nobody entirely escapes! That is the human condition. All great leaders will experience some form of adversity. Their resilience will determine whether they can overcome the challenges on their way to building a winning life.

Resilience means the ability to rebound, recoil, or spring back to the original form or position. In the context of leadership it means the capacity to recover from often traumatically adverse life events (illness, death, divorce, catastrophic events, for example) and go on to achieve eventual restoration or improvement, further increasing the capacity to withstand chronic stress and adverse life considerations

NATIONAL TRAGEDIES—WHY

Ever since 9/11, we all realize we live in a different world. The business world has experienced unheard-of losses ranging from the Ponzi schemes of Madoff to the biggest global financial meltdown in seventy years to shootings and international disasters. In sports, we saw the bizarre shooting and murder of a basketball player at Baylor in 2003 and a coach who reacted poorly, resulting in sanctions. Baylor has resiliently bounced back with a great coach in Scott Drew, age thirty-three at the time of his hire, to become one of the top teams in the Big XII and make it to the Sweet Sixteen in 2010.

TEAM-TO-DYNASTY TIP #13. Never underestimate the depth to which some people will stoop to to disparage your reputation, if they are envious of your accomplishments or the position you espouse. Every great leader will have detractors. Evil exists in human nature, and when others cannot defeat you, they may spread rumors or attack your character. Don't stoop to their insecure, petty level. Simply outlast them.

I realized just how much things had changed when, on the second anniversary of the Columbine school shootings, I was invited to work with a number of churches and family members who were impacted. Keep in mind that this was the wealthiest school district in the country. And the young shooters came from affluent, intact professional families. Upon arriving at a local church, I spent most of the first day meeting one-on-one with ministers in nearby parishes. They were also traumatized. In addition, I gave a talk to families at a large church and was interviewed there by the local TV station before the event. When it came time for me to speak, I noticed that the TV crew had not left. I asked why they were staying, and they told me they had hired a psychologist to work with the TV station and wanted to hear me speak! Everyone was traumatized.

The Lutheran ministers were struggling to keep their congregations together, especially one minister, who had buried one of the shooters. I also visited a family whose daughter had been shot and paralyzed; her mother later committed suicide because of the hurt. You see, these examples remind all of us that we will be tested—either personally or professionally—and that our success will be determined by our core ability to be resilient.

MIT management guru Yossi Sheffi (and author of *The Resilient Enterprise*) indicates that good leaders know what to do when things go wrong. Great leaders even anticipate problems before they happen.

HENDRICK MOTORSPORTS

In 2002, I became the team psychologist for Hendrick Motorsports and have enjoyed working there ever since. The national sports media recently voted it the greatest motorsports team ever and the seventh-best sports-team dynasty of all time. Why? Because of its owner, Rick Hendrick! His character! The leadership model presented below explains how he and his team could achieve such a lofty status. They are best known for their chief characteristic of resilience. Resilience epitomizes this man and his entire organization.

THE RESILIENCE TEST

It was 10:30 on Sunday morning in October 2004—the fall Martinsville race weekend. I noticed I had missed a call on my cell phone. When I listened to the message, I found out it was Ricky Hendrick, Rick's son—"Jack, this is Ricky. Please give me a call. I have something I need to talk with you about." I thought I would wait until after church and after the race to call him back, since I figured he was already at the track and getting ready to "spot" the race for his driver Brian Vickers. (A critical role for every driver is to get constant communication from his spotter as to the cars all around him and where to drive his car if there is a wreck.) It was the last phone call he would ever make.

Ricky was very special to me and just about everyone else. He had his daddy's smarts, but was way more charismatic. His good looks, blonde hair, and blue eyes, along with the perfect smile, could light up a room. He knew everyone's name and charmed them all. Most of all, he had fun. He did things his way—he always wore casual dress, with flip-flops and a backwards cap. It was his way perhaps of distinguishing himself from his legendary father, who knows the importance of the corporate button-down sponsorship world he cultivates. Bad weather led to a tragedy beyond belief when the Hendrick corporate plane crashed into a mountain. Rick was also supposed to be on the plane but wasn't feeling well and was not able to travel. He lost his only son—whom he loved so deeply. Ricky idolized his father and was never as happy as when he was driving one of Rick's racecars to victory lane.

That would have been enough of a tragedy, but also on the plane were Rick's brother, his two nieces, his chief engineer/engine builder, and his longtime general manager, in addition to a DuPont executive and two of his longtime pilots. It was the worst professional tragedy of my career. All these years later, I still find it hard to believe it could happen. I still see Ricky's face, his smile, his beaming blue eyes, and his energy. Why! Why do bad things happen to good people?

For much of the next twelve months I switched from being a performance/sports psychologist to being a clinical psychologist helping the employees of the organization who were shaken by this experience.

Many of us marvel at how Rick could go on. *Resilience* is a word that best captures his personality and perhaps epitomizes the secret to his success in building the greatest motorsports dynasty of all time.

No one would have blamed him if he had decided to sell the organization or stop going to races, but that's not Rick. He wanted to be there for his employees as the entire NASCAR nation mourned for its most respected leader. Rick's resilience facing the worst situation a parent can face, his optimism, his hope, and his confidence remain steadfast. He will say he has been able to move on because of all the support he received from the people he has cared for over the years. Those who work for him have countless stories of how he stepped up for them when they most needed it. He has built a legacy of loyal followers that is unrivaled in his business, and many of his devoted customers double as fans.

This is the second tragedy he is overcoming. In 1996, he was diagnosed with leukemia and underwent an exhaustive treatment program. Now in remission, he has formed the Hendrick Marrow Program, to which he generously contributes and promotes.

HUMBLE BEGINNINGS

In his early sixties now, Rick Hendrick grew up on a family farm near the small town of South Hill, Virginia, in a close-knit tobacco community. His father, mentor, and best friend, known to everyone in motorsports as "Papa Joe," took him to the races on weekends. Rick started working on cars at age five and quickly became a "gear head." He built his first car, a 1931 Chevy, at age fourteen and soon set drag-racing records. The following year Rick won a statewide engine-building contest. A gifted athlete at Park View High School, he turned down a professional baseball career with the Pirates to attend North Carolina State University on a work-study program with Western Electric. Apparently he was too talented to finish his engineering degree. He bought and fixed an Opal for $350 and sold it for $1, 000 a few days later, thus launching his career in the car-selling business. Soon after, at age twenty five, he was selected to be the general manager of a Chevrolet dealership in Bennettsville, South Carolina, making him the youngest Chevrolet dealer in the United States at the time.

Over the past thirty-five years, Rick's phenomenal leadership and business skills have allowed him to establish one of the top auto retail operations in the county. The Hendrick Automotive Group (HAG) is currently ranked by *Ward's Dealer Business* magazine as the sixth-largest megadealer based on sales in excess of $4 billion and 100,000 units per year. HAG operates 80 automobile and truck dealerships and 13 collision centers from the Carolinas to California. The HAG employs more than five thousand individuals headquartered in the Charlotte, North Carolina, area. As NASCAR has grown, so too has the HAG.

THE HENDRICK DYNASTY

Rick Hendrick quickly became successful in the world of motorsports. He competed in boat racing in his late twenties and soon set a world speed record at 222.2 miles per hour in his boat *Nitro Fever*. He won three consecutive national championships in 1981, 1982, and 1983. Following the death of his friend in a race, Rick ended his boat racing career. He then directed his passion to building his first NASCAR team in 1984.

As CEO of Hendrick Motorsports, Rick oversees 550 employees on a one hundred-acre campus with 500,000 square feet of work space and close to $150 million in revenue yearly. It is rated as the top NASCAR racing organization, valued at over $400 million. As far as dynasties go, the Hendrick organization was ranked as the seventh-best sports dynasty of all time. We all realized what an amazing honor it is to work for this organization and for Mr. Hendrick.

In all, Hendrick Motorsports has garnered nine NASCAR Cup Series championships, one NASCAR Nationwide Series championship, and three NASCAR Craftsman Truck Series championships, making it one of stock-car racing's premier organizations. Mr. Hendrick is just the second team owner in NASCAR's modern era to earn more than two hundred Cup Series victories.

His local leadership in Charlotte involves being one of four partners who founded the Charlotte Hornets team in the NBA, as well as establishing the NASCAR Museum in Charlotte, a huge $100 million attraction.

THE LEADER WITHIN

Although Hendrick has built an extremely successful organization and gained global recognition for his efforts on and off the track, he admittedly has not done it alone. He repeatedly gives credit to his employees for the personal success he has enjoyed. His employees talk about Rick as the very best leader in the industry, bar none.

In every conversation I have had in a series of interviews and casual conversations with Rick and his employees across the Hendrick Motorsports campus since 2002, the descriptions of Rick are 100 percent consistent—he is genuine; he is authentic; he is a resilient winner. Perhaps this is why Rick was chosen among hundreds of other possible choices for the prestigious Horatio Alger Association of Distinguished Americans award in 2006. Rick simply stands out above the pack and gets deserved credit for his confident, caring, inspiring, and visionary leadership in this fast-paced, fast-growing business.

"In everything we do, whether business or sports, we're basically in the people business," he said. "We've built a good team, and it's the team that accomplishes the goal." For Rick, the core of business is about building vital relationships and friendships. In the interviews, everyone said that he is someone you can count on to back you up but also to take you on if you don't behave professionally. The Hendrick dynasty has had great leaders at the top of the organization and on each team.

Rick has spread his leadership and cultural DNA everywhere with employees and customers. When speaking to his employees, you will clearly hear what Rick emphasizes: the importance of vision and values. He does what great leaders have done throughout history in that he makes his associates feel that they are meaningful and that what they are doing is important. The employees loved his late father, "Papa Joe," and his charismatic son Ricky just as much, so they cling to his caring support.

RESILIENCE THROUGH TEAMWORK

"Teamwork" is Rick's mantra. He rewards his staff for working together as a team. He personally shakes the hands of each of his five thousand employees on the automotive side each year as he visits numerous deal-erships. An employee who has twenty years with the company gets a $10,000 Rolex watch—seventy-five employees received one last year. The fringe benefits, retirement packages, and bonuses (those who meet their goals get $1,000; others are paid weekly bonuses) are the most generous in all of NASCAR and among automotive dealerships. That is why Rick's turnover rate is a fraction of what other NASCAR owners and car dealer-ships experience. At Hendrick Motorsports, all the employees gather for a lunch each quarter where they can win more than $10,000 in prizes.

"People know where my heart is, and what my core is, and they know it's a pretty simple philosophy. They know I want to win. They have the same heart that I have. We may not always have the same values, but we have the same heart. All you have to do is take care of the people. People know the difference they can make, they know the decisions that have to be made, and I let them make those decisions—but they know that I'll back them up if need be.

"The motorsports business is all about winning—not about profit. We are graded by how many wins we achieve. Record books say you won or lost. You need to decide how you are going to win. We try to select the right people and get them to work together."

Ken Howes is Rick's longtime Director of Competition. His job is to pull off something that's unique in the motorsports world and in any other sports. Teams at Hendrick Motorsports vigorously compete with each other on the weekends, but during the week they work together, learn from each other, and share top-secret set-up information to gain the extra edge. It is an innovative, technology-driven company that emphasizes treating its people better than other companies do. If you ask the crew chiefs or the drivers Jeff Gordon, Jimmie Johnson, Dale Earnhardt, Jr., and Kasey Kahne, they will tell you that Rick is like a father to them. They don't want to let him down, so they try to please the motivator. They believe they owe their successes to Rick, who has taught them the importance of building a winning dynasty that will last a long time. It is a winning formula that will last a lifetime for each of them.

On the automotive side, Rick believes in taking care of employees first so that they will then take care of customers. He has five criteria for success on the automotive side:

»   Good location   »   Good facility

»   Good market   »   Good franchise

»   Good people

Mr. Hendrick believes that if you lose any one of these you will be okay, but not great. If you leave out two of them, you won't make it.

He is customer-centric and has a unique rule: If a customer's complaint makes it all the way up to him, that customer gets his or her request free—whatever it is—and sometimes that means a new car.

THE NASCAR PHENOMENON

Millions attend, millions watch on TV, all enjoying the fastest-growing spectator sport in America. NASCAR is the most popular spectator sport and the second most televised sport.

NASCAR's fan base is over 75 million, a fourth of the population of the United States. Some six to ten million fans from coast to coast watch each of the season's thirty-six races.

Average attendance per race is approximately 110,000. That is more than the Super Bowl, the NBA finals, and the World Series.

Of the top twenty sporting events most attended by fans in the United State annually, seventeen are NASCAR events.

Races are televised to more than 115 countries.

NASCAR has a six-year, $2.4 billion television contract with NBC, Fox, and ESPN.

The annual revenue in licensed NASCAR products alone is at $3 billion.

A recent Gallup poll revealed that a full 28 percent of Americans are tried-and-true race fans, with 38 percent of this total being women (and growing fast). Some 53 percent of the fans work in professional, managerial, or skilled labor positions, with a median yearly household income of $50,000. If you thought the majority of NASCAR fans were a bunch of folks who like to work in their garages on Saturday night and drink beer—you'd be way off.

BRIAN VICKERS—NASCAR CHAMPION

The first time I met Brian Vickers all I could think about was *Butch Cassidy and the Sundance Kid* with Paul Newman and Robert Redford. These two bank-robbing bandits were chased clear into South America by the Pinkerton boys. Unable to shake them, the outlaws keep looking over their shoulders only to see that no matter what, they kept coming. Their classic line, often quoted, was "Who are those guys?" Well, that's what I kept saying to myself about Brian—"Who is this guy?" I first met him at a NASCAR race when he was just eighteen years old and driving for

Hendrick Motorsports in what was then called the Busch Series. He was in the hauler (large semi-truck that carries the two race cars and lots of gear). I introduced myself as the sports psychologist for the team, and the next thing I knew two hours had gone by during which he asked me questions in machine-gun fashion about the genetics-versus-nature aspects of development and other intellectual questions. His personality blew me away. *Who is this guy?* I kept asking myself.

I have been privileged to work closely with well over a thousand collegiate athletes and more than three hundred at the pro level in all the major sports, but nobody—and I mean nobody—had ever asked me such penetrating questions. I knew he was special from that very first interaction.

A few months later I had dinner with Brian and his parents, Clyde and Ramona, and told them that I was blown away by this bright young man and that, if they would trust me, I would like to mentor him.

It has turned out to be the most special relationship I have ever had with an athlete. He is like a son to me and never ceases to amaze me.

Brian was youngest driver to win the Busch Series championship at age twenty. In 2009 at age twenty six, he made the NASCAR Chase, which includes the top twelve drivers in the NASCAR Cup Series, and he is recognized as a future top-five driver. It was a tall order to make the Chase with the Red Bull Team, in existence only three years. Brian is very bright and passionate about life, with an astonishing desire to learn. He is mature beyond his age, but what stands out most is his resilience. His ability to handle life's tragedies was tested twice when he lost his two best friends—by the age of twenty. Adam Petty (grandson of the famed Richard Petty) was killed in a crash at a track. While they were close, his very best friend and the person who gave him his biggest break, by giving him a ride in NASCAR's elite level, was Ricky Hendrick.

Ricky Hendrick lived with Brian, they traveled together, and Ricky was Brian's spotter at the races. In the years since the plane crash, it has taken a great deal of resilience for Brian to go to Martinsville each year and race, knowing the sport you love so much has taken even more. The plane crash occurred on Brian's twenty-first birthday.

Additional resilience was apparent when, at age twenty six, Brian nearly died from blood clots and missed half of an entire season, unable to drive while taking medications.

Chapter 5

DYNASTIC LEADERS
ARE ANALYTICAL

Now this is the Law of the Jungle—as old and as true as the sky;
And the Wolf that shall keep it may prosper, but the Wolf that shall
break it must die.
As the creeper that girdles the tree-trunk the Law runneth forward
and back—
For the strength of the Pack is the Wolf, and the strength of the Wolf is
the Pack.   —Rudyard Kipling

This quotation hangs on the locker-room wall of the University of Syracuse football team. I consulted with the entire team and coaching staff on a number of occasions to build team unity, as I do with numerous sports teams and corporations around the country. They liked this quote that I borrowed from Phil Jackson, who used it with his "Jordan teams" at the Bulls.

It speaks to the issue of how a leader needs his team and how the team needs its leader. It has always been that way and always will be—a law of human behavior.

The fifth personality trait—analytical or integrative thinking—involves the ability to problem solve, to analyze all the data and come up with the right solutions. A deeper understanding of this trait will assist us to better build a team into a dynasty.

Why an entire chapter on the importance of the leadership personality trait of being analytical?

Leadership has evolved from the importance of raw intelligence. In the 1940s, '50s and '60s, those with the highest raw IQ were often promoted to CEOs. Many of the CEOs had engineering degrees, the most popular major for the brightest students. Screening for leaders included a battery of IQ tests (usually the Wechsler or Stanford-Binet test, which were popular at that time).

Today we know that a high IQ, while helpful, is less important than wisdom, or the ability to effectively problem solve.

We have all seen some very bright people who were missing that ability to tap into their intellect to solve complex problems.

Leaders have gone from not having enough data to make decisions to being overwhelmed with all the information that, today, is so easily available.

Whether in business or in sports, the leader and a few chosen assistants determine winning and losing, a dynasty's success or failure. It's always the people at the top. If they have flaws, they will not succeed very well or for very long. It's the strength of the lead wolf and the pack that follows.

So much of our happiness today is determined more than ever by the people who lead us. Who does lead us? Our government, our employers, our religious leaders, our teachers, those who impact our lives on a daily basis, and even the teams we root for—all influence our individual culture.

The top decision-makers I interview today lament the same thing everywhere—"Where have all the leaders gone?" Our country and indeed the world at large is lacking leaders. Why? Well, it turns out that (1) some potential leaders prefer to put their families first; (2) leadership today means exposure to media scrutiny and loss of personal privacy; and (3) perhaps most compelling of all, it's harder now to be a leader.

Wisdom is required, as well as a new way of thinking.

LEADERSHIP CHALLENGES

Consider this: The average American takes in thirty-four gigabytes of data daily. This is an increase of 350 percent over the last thirty years. This consists of 100,000 words from TV, radio, the Web, and the print media. We watch five hours of TV, listen to two hours of radio, use our computer for two hours, play video games for one hour and read for thirty-six minutes—each day! OMG!

No wonder we are a stressed-out nation.

And guess what? It's going to get worse! We are flooded with data. It's not that we don't get enough information; it's often that there is too much.

In 2005, a gigabyte cost $43. In 2016 a gigabyte is projected to cost 10¢. We can now put on one flash drive 256 GB, or the equivalent of 186,000 floppies or three hundred CDs—pretty staggering when you think about it.

It is difficult to sift through all this information now and make wise decisions. The slightest failure is instantly known and broadcast for all to see. Think of the visual image of the leaking oil well on the twenty-four-hour news or a blown call at the World Cup by a referee repeated on every sports channel for weeks.

TEAM-TO-DYNASTY TIP #14. "A man may die, nations may rise and fall, but an idea lives on." —John F. Kennedy

National surveys have repeatedly indicated that what people want most out of their leaders is, first, honesty and, second, vision. What do we mean by vision? It has changed dramatically from the eras of Vince Lombardi and General George Patton, when leadership was a command-and-control model. Coaches and bosses told people what to do and everyone followed.

People today want to know WHY? (Why are we going in a certain direction) and WHERE? (Where will we go and how will we know when we are there?) Vision is more than a clear picture of a goal—it involves a different type of thinking. It's not just high IQ, although that generally helps, but an analytical process based on a different way of thinking. We clearly observe this in the following explanation of the Buffett-Munger-Sokol approach, in which thinking traits help explain the success of Bershire Hathaway.

THE ANALYTICAL MIND

Roger Martin, dean of the highly ranked Rotman School of Management at the University of Toronto, gives us insight into how a leader thinks in his aptly titled book *How Successful Leaders Think*. He notes that leaders of dynasties have had to adapt and change, and that fact alone makes it difficult to copy their actions. He refers to this process as "integrative thinking," the trait of great leaders involving the capacity to hold in their heads two opposite ideas at once—while generating a new idea that combines the elements of both into a superior new one. Along with the inductive/ deductive method of thinking, integrative thinking separates the extraordinary thinkers from those who are mediocre.

In his book *The Opposable Mind*, Martin acknowledges that it's not a new idea—F. Scott Fitzgerald, more than sixty years ago, saw "the ability to hold two opposing ideas in mind at the same time and still retain the ability to function" as a sign of a "first-rate intelligence."

CONVENTIONAL VERSUS INTEGRATIVE THINKING

When responding to problems or challenges, dynastic leaders tend to possess integrative thinking skills. Those who are conventional thinkers seek simplicity along the way and are often forced to make unattractive trade-offs. The conventional approach results in linear thinking, breaking problems into pieces and working on issues separately and sequentially.

The Japan nuclear disaster of 2011 is a perfect example of how flawed and inadequate this approach can be. Tokyo Electric Power Company tried to sequentially solve the problems in a step-like format. You sometimes have to attack the problem at multiple angles, all at once; you can't wait to solve multiple problems one at a time. It takes too long and creates more problems to address. By contrast, integrative thinkers welcome complexity—even if it means repeating one or more of the steps—and this allows them to craft innovative solutions.

BAD ANALYTICAL SKILLS

Many bad decisions have been made by failed leaders or would-be leaders due to their inability to problem-solve while also exhibiting other deficits of personality traits. The demise of some of the great dynasties in sports and in business can be traced to this. It is stunning to see how fast this can happen. In the corporate world, the classic example is the dot-com bust and the demise of Enron, recognized at the time as "the best-run company in America" by all sorts of publications. Jeff Skilling, the former CEO, graduated in the top 5 percent of his classes at Harvard and had a Ph.D. in engineering; his cohort was labeled "the smartest guy in the room" in a couple of best-selling books. They are now all in jail!

HEROIC MILITARY LEADERS

The greatest leaders in the history of civilization have always been integrative thinkers who often could outwit others despite the odds. From 500 BC to the twentieth century, much of leadership was defined by heroic or military leaders.

SUN TZU

Perhaps the greatest military leader of all time was the Chinese warrior and philosopher Sun Tzu (544 BC–496 BC). His name was a title of honor given to his real name of Sun Wu—the word *Wu* meaning military. Sun Tzu wrote his book *The Art of War* 2,500 years ago. It is still taught in military war colleges and in core curriculums of business, politics, and sports courses today. Key executives at many Japanese companies are required to read it. This frequently referenced book was written on bamboo strips and is made up of thirteen chapters. The three key principles:

> » If you know your enemies and know yourself, you will not be
> imperiled in a hundred battles. If you do not know your enemies

but do know yourself, you will win one and lose one. If you do not know your enemies or yourself, you will be imperiled in every single battle.

» To win one hundred victories in one hundred battles is not the ultimate skill; to subdue the enemy without fighting is the ultimate skill.

» Avoid your enemies' strong positions and attack their weak positions.

Sun Tzu effectively employed these principles when he took his thirty thousand Wu warriors against the 300,000-strong enemy in the nearby state of Chu. Using his intelligence, cunning, and strategies, he defeated his enemies. Sun Tzu wrote, "The winning army realizes the conditions for victory first and then fights; the losing army fights first, and then seeks victory." Following Sun Tzu's tactics proved to be the perfect strategy on June 6, 1944, during the D-Day landings at Normandy, during the decisive June 1942 Battle of Midway, and near the end of World War II at the Battle of the Bulge at Bastogne. At Midway Atoll, Admiral Nimitz set a trap, destroyed four aircraft carriers, and turned the tide of the war against the Japanese. General Patton pulled his armored division out of battle, marched 140 miles in the middle of the winter in the opposite direction, with no rest or hot food, to barely save the 101st Airborne Division at the besieged city of Bastogne and save the march toward Germany.

General Robert E. Lee, considered by many to be one of the best military leaders of his time, failed to follow the principles of Sun Tzu. He suffered a terrible loss of lives at Gettysburg. Similar fate befell some American forces during the Vietnam War when our superior forces were unable to totally overpower a smaller guerrilla force.

ALEXANDER THE GREAT

Alexander the Great (356 BC–323 BC) was the greatest heroic leader ever. He had conquered the world by the time of his death at the early age of thirty two. We can clearly see the leadership model used during Alexander's reign.

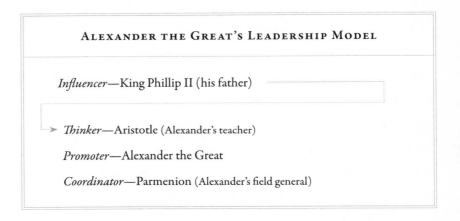

ALEXANDER THE GREAT'S LEADERSHIP MODEL

Influencer—King Phillip II (his father)

Thinker—Aristotle (Alexander's teacher)

Promoter—Alexander the Great

Coordinator—Parmenion (Alexander's field general)

Three of the greatest thinkers of all time—Socrates, Plato, and Aristotle—each influenced his behavior. As the greatest philosopher of all time, Aristotle greatly influenced young Alexander to think integratively, and Alexander applied that principle to his first great battle. After his father was assassinated, he became king of Macedon, a region in northern Greece. The Boy-King, as he was called, had conquered Greece by the time he was 20 years old, after first serving as cavalry commander at the age of 16. In 331 BC, Alexander turned his attention to the largest kingdom in the world—the Persian Empire. His character and innovative thinking led him to the decisive battle of Gaugamela, the greatest battle of the ancient world. Against the King of Persia's army of 250,000, Alexander arrayed his army of 47,000 men. Employing new tactical maneuvers and formations, Alexander's strategic analysis, which was against the advice of his conservative general, Parmenion, soundly routed the Persians and conquered the entire ancient world. The story of Alexander the Great is the perfect example of the model, process, and traits of a dynastic leader who effectively used the P4 formula that was the best in the world at the time and has endured for more than two thousand years. It is a model that still works today.

All great leaders, from ancient times to the present, were great strategists, problem solvers who could harness their analytical skills to outsmart their competition. Analytical skills are a crucial personality trait for those who want to win.

FOUR ERAS OF LEADERSHIP

Insightful research by Harvard Business School professor Rakesh Khurana sees recent leadership as having four distinct eras:

FIRST ERA—BUILDER CEO—1880–1920. Focus on building a large company, e.g., Rockefeller and Goodrich.

SECOND ERA—ORGANIZATIONAL CEO—1920–1980. Focus on building the organization, e.g., GM and GE.

THIRD ERA—VISIONARY CEO—1980–2010. Focus on responsibility of business to increase profit, e.g., Iacocca and Welch.

FOURTH ERA—LEGISLATIVE CEO—2010–2030. Focus on a new type of leader who can look beyond the short-term vision and inspire others in an era of regulatory control (Reingold, 2008).

ERA OF ECONOMIC UNCERTAINTY

More regulatory control resulting from the financial meltdown of 2008–2010 will dominate all teams in the future. The impact on business and even sports teams will require very savvy leadership skills.

Ram Charon, in his book *Leadership in the Era of Economic Uncertainty*, emphasizes a new approach—management intensity—a deep immersion in the operational details of a business and the outside world combined with a hands-on involvement and follow-through. Charon asserts that a leader's ability, when trouble appears, to act decisively on the basis of up-to-date information that is unfiltered, as well as that person's daily high visibility and interaction, will be essential for going forward as a successful leader of any team.

Thank goodness leadership has evolved from the buzzwords of "thinking out of the box," "new paradigm," and "transparency" and the passing fads. This is no doubt due to the demands of the media—TV, print, Internet, blogs, Twitter, etc.—for more accountability.

AMERICA'S MOST ADMIRED COMPANIES

The analytical trait is found in particular among the most admired companies in America, many from the technology sector, due to their innovative and creative ability to think differently—integratively! The top three companies ranked in 2011 by *Fortune* magazine's survey of the Fortune 500 companies are (1) Apple, (2) Berkshire Hathaway and (3) General Electric.

Let's look at each of these three companies in order to best capture how they were able to achieve this status and perhaps give us insight into how that can be replicated.

APPLE TEAM

Apple is the most admired company both globally and in America. This thirty-two-year-old company represents the most successful marriage of design and business, with $32 billion in annual sales. The makers of the iMac, iPod, iPhone, and iPad have revolutionized the technology world mainly as a result of their ability to understand the interplay between design and manufacturing.

Apple, led by CEO Steve Jobs, created a new business model by using a branding process that has resulted in breathtaking growth and by dreaming up products so new and ingenious that the consumer electronics industry, the record industry, the movie industry, and video and music production businesses have been revolutionized. The return of the brilliant Jobs during the last decade has propelled Apple to the number-one spot among Fortune 500 companies for total return to shareholders over the past five years of more than 100 percent and more than 50 percent for the past ten years—far ahead of the market benchmark—and shows no sign of slowing down. The key to Apple's winning formula with its particularly respected analytical skills is the teamwork of its unique workforce of 25,000 employees with an emphasis on collaboration and organization by both product and function.

APPLE MODEL

» *Promoter*—Steve Jobs, chairman & former CEO

» *Thinker*—Jonathon Ive, senior VP of industrial design
(and Robert Brunner before him)

» *Coordinator*—Tim Cook, CEO

Apple's management philosophy is the opposite of most businesses, which espouse diversification and spread themselves too thin, making too many products to defuse risk and in the process getting mired in mediocrity. Apple's approach is to put every resource into just a few, but very good, products. Jobs pushes his company to think differently labelling himself as the company's "Creator-in-Chief," which extends to everything the company does, from products to ad campaigns (Morris, 2008).

GENERAL ELECTRIC MODEL

Jack Welch began his career with General Electric Company in 1960. In 1981, he became the company's chairman and CEO. During his tenure, GE's market capitalization increased by $400 billion, making it the world's most valuable corporation. Welch's "no-excuse, get-it-done, straight-from-the-gut" approach, his insights and original thinking on how to actually run programs and business, are a great example of taking a team to a dynasty level. He stresses the four "E's" of leadership—edge, execution, energy, and the ability to energize others.

In addition to these three companies, leaders I have interviewed over the years have frequently mentioned examples of very talented, analytical leaders who have founded or led innovative companies:

- » *Ford*—Alan Mulally, CEO
- » *Cisco*—John Chambers, CEO
- » *Xerox*—Anne Mulcahy, CEO
- » *Johnson & Johnson*—Bill Weldon, CEO
- » *Google*—Eric Schmidt, CEO, & Sergey Brin and Larry Page, founders

» *Procter & Gamble*—Alan Lafley, former CEO

» *Amazon*—Jeffrey Bezos, CEO

» *Nucor*—Daniel DiMicco, CEO

BERKSHIRE HATHAWAY:
THE BEST THINKERS IN THE WORLD

Warren Buffett—THE PROMOTER

The integrative or analytical thinking personality trait is perhaps best understood when applied to Buffett's team and his Berkshire Hathaway company. It is a unique way of explaining the company's success and serves as a model for others to follow

Insight into what makes a great leader can be traced back to one's childhood. Warren grew up a quiet and humble young man, having learned his entrepreneurial skills in his grandfather's grocery store as a clerk. There were hard times for the family during the Depression; Warren was born ten months after the crash. His parents' work ethic and caring prompted him to say he won the "Ovarian Lottery," as he could not have had better parents. The only son and middle child began earning money early on by delivering newspapers, selling six-packs of Coke and making a nickel for each sale, and hiring his friends to retrieve golf balls in the golf course lake and reselling them at a profit. In ninth grade, he bought used pinball machines and placed them in barbershops around town. He attended Omaha public schools and graduated in 1947 in Washington, DC, after his father was elected to Congress.

TEAM-TO-DYNASTY TIP #15. Warren Buffett's philosophy: Rule #1—Never lose money. Rule #2—Never forget Rule #1.

Buffett first enrolled at Wharton and after two years went to the University of Nebraska, graduating in 1951 with a BS in economics. After an interviewer in Chicago did not think he was Harvard material, he received his MS in economics at Columbia Business School, studying under the brilliant Benjamin Graham and David Doss. Graham had a profound influence on Warren with his beliefs in value investing—which is to look at stocks as a businesses, while seeking a margin of safety by using the market's fluctuations to one's advantage, an approach that will never go away! He returned to Omaha, got married, had three children, and worked a few years for Benjamin Graham. In 1959, he met Charlie Munger and opened numerous partnerships. In 1960, he asked a doctor, friend, and partner to find others to invest. All totaled, eleven physicians agreed, and now that initial investment is worth hundreds of millions.

A former colleague of mine and fellow researcher in the Department of Pediatrics at the University of Nebraska Medical Center, where we were on the faculty together, was one of the original investors along with her husband. I was honored to publish with this brilliant lady, who helped start poison control centers in America at hospitals for children. Her small initial investment in Berkshire Hathaway stock has grown to be worth an estimated half a billion dollars in Buffett stock. All told, billions in legacy funds now exist with these physicians and businesspeople with ties to Omaha. They have all generously contributed to the Omaha community.

The Purchase of Berkshire Hathaway

By 1962, Buffett became a millionaire from his partnerships and collapsed all of them into one company—a textile manufacturing firm named Berkshire Hathaway—and kept the title over the years. Today his stock fluctuates between $60 to $70 billion, making him among the wealthiest men in the world alternating at the top spot with his dear friend and intellectual match Bill Gates. Today, Buffett is the quintessential Promoter—the man most quoted, admired, respected, and interviewed by the media. It's not just his financial accomplishments that have made him the all-time greatest investor; it's also his leadership skills. He bailed out Solomon Brothers in 1990 during their financial crisis when a rogue broker was guilty of bid rigging. Buffett came in and studied the company that he owned 12 percent of. He replaced the CEO himself and held together not only the company, but also the entire U.S. stock market, which was on shaky footing.

TEAM-TO-DYNASTY TIP #16. When handling a crisis, make your mantra, "Go fast, go hard, and go long!"

When handling a crisis, be Warren Buffett! Hold a press conference immediately; answer every question for as long as it takes. That is what Warren did when that rogue trader almost brought down Solomon Brothers. Warren quickly called a press conference and answered every single question from every reporter until the last one went home. A crisis was averted. If you follow Buffett's example it's all over in a few hours, as opposed to front-page headlines every day for sometimes weeks, repeating the crisis, which can destroy a team, a company, or a dynasty. Go fast! Go hard! Go long! This is the mantra for handling a crisis.

This crisis repeated itself with General Re and the forced resignation of Maurice Greenberg at AIG in 2006, resulting in a fine of $1.6 billion. In each of these situations, Buffett's honesty and integrity saved the company and the potential loss of confidence in our entire financial systems. He has now become the White Knight who companies rely on to help and save them because of the respect he commands and his brand image. The "Sage of Omaha" exhibits all of the personality traits necessary for a dynastic leader, but particularly analytical skill, making him one of the most remarkable leaders I have ever met, along with his partner Munger.

CHARLIE MUNGER—THE THINKER

Although Buffett has played all three roles—Promoter, Thinker, and Coordinator—early in his career, he later added a Thinker, or at least a Co-Thinker, to his inner circle. Interestingly, Charlie Munger also grew up in Omaha, attending Omaha Central High School. His nickname was "Brains." Charlie later met Warren when he was in his mid-twenties. Also interesting, Charlie (who did not know Warren as a child) had once worked for Warren's grandfather at the Buffett & Sons Grocery Store. Munger immediately took to Buffett, recognizing his talent.

Warren Buffett and Charlie Munger are two of the brightest people I have ever met in my life. Not because of high IQ, although it's high; it's their ability to problem solve that is so impressive! The problem today is not that there is a lack of enough data; there is perhaps too much information. People can't "data mine" and pull out the key data points for decision making, or their cognitive problem-solving skills are flawed. It is fascinating to see how a brilliant economist and lawyer and the CEOs of each of their companies can come together to problem solve—each of them with his or her own unique problem-solving styles and personalities.

Charlie, in his mid-eighties, is vice chairman of Berkshire Hathaway and loves playing the role of the curmudgeon who frowns on most investment ideas. "When I call Charlie with an idea," Buffett has stated, "and he says, 'That is a really dumb idea,' that means we should put 100 percent of our net worth into it. If he says, 'That is the dumbest thing I've ever heard,' then you should put 50 percent of our net worth into it. Only if he says, 'I'm going to have you committed,'" does it mean he really doesn't like the idea." This Johnny Carson-Ed McMahon-type relationship started in 1959 and has continued through to the present with the most remarkable financial growth for a company anywhere in the world.

Charlie attended the University of Michigan after growing up in Omaha. He also went to Cal Tech and the U.S. Army Air Corps before entering Harvard Law School, graduating in 1948 magna cum laude. He started his own law firm and focused on real estate until 1965, when he left to concentrate on managing his investments. He is chairman of Wesco Financial Corporation, which is now owned by Berkshire Hathaway. A multibillionaire himself, Munger has also donated a great deal of his wealth, but does not devote as much of his time to the day-to-day operations of Berkshire Hathaway.

What distinguishes these two leaders, particularly Charlie, is their intellectual curiosity. His hero is Benjamin Franklin, but he has read everything from Cicero and Maimonides to Pierre de Fermat and Pascal. He is big on mathematical models—quantitative methods and decision trees. He uses multiple disciplines to apply the mental models that he feels are critical to his success. Munger has been influenced, as he states, more by Robert Cialdini than by any other scientist. Cialdini is a social psychologist who has published the very best works on human persuasion and the psychology of misjudgment. Munger states, "Terribly smart people make totally bonkers mistakes by failing to pay heed." (Munger, 1995).

CHARLIE MUNGER'S MENTAL MODELS

Charlie considers the psychology of misjudgment as critical to a person's success, since a person's mind can be manipulated in amazing ways. He quotes Pascal: "The mind of man at one and the same time is both the glory and the shame of the universe." We reach wrong conclusions based on manipulations, self-delusions, and ego trips.

Charlie believes it is necessary to follow a two-track analysis—rational considerations that govern interests and the subconscious influences, which can be useful, but which often malfunction. Charlie bought into the whole concept of behavioral economics long before it became popular. In a nutshell, behavioral economics looks at the *why* of investment behavior, which is often irrational—what investment talking heads call "the psychology of the market."

Charlie's book *Poor Charlie's Almanack* (2005) introduced the concept of "Elementary Worldly Wisdom" as it relates to business and finance. His worldly wisdom consists of a set of mental models framed as a latticework to help solve the problems of business. Charlie feels that eighty to ninety models will help a person make really wise decisions and best understand how biases and incentives affect human behavior. (For a more complete analysis, see an excellent book by Peter Bevelin, *Seeking Wisdom*).

THE BUFFETT-MUNGER MIND

It is no accident that this duo has become the best pair of financial investment and business minds in the last fifty years. They are, as Munger describes them, "learning machines," and they work hard, have passion, and are smart. But close analysis indicates a very rare cognitive process employed by these two individuals. Drawing from the fields of cognitive psychology, analytical logic, and the epistemology training I received but struggled with, I have concluded it is really their unique problem-solving skills that allow them to possess what we label today as "breakthrough thinking." They effectively utilize an inductive thinking process to problem solve.

A sports analogy helps to explain this process. The Olympic sport of high-jumping reached its height of popularity in the 1960s when the seven-foot barrier was broken. Everyone used the same technique with slight variations. A jumper would run at the bar, kick his front leg up over it, and roll the rest of his body over the bar. But after the seven-foot barrier was broken, gains were miniscule until "breakthrough thinking" totally reversed the process. An athlete named Dick Fosbury tried something radically different. He ran at the bar, threw his upper body over the bar—backwards—and yanked his legs over on his way down. In the 1968 Summer Olympics, he broke the record and won a gold medal. Since then everyone has jumped this reverse way after hundreds of years the old way. Fosbury—whose technique became known as the "Fosbury Flop"— employed inductive reasoning, although I am sure he would say he was just being creative.

THE INDUCTIVE & DEDUCTIVE PROCESSES

INDUCTION

Step 1

When making a decision, you go inside your mind first. You pull from all your experiences and memories of the past, all your learning, reading, listening, and observations, and come up with a solution based upon this internal process.

Step 2

After you have decided upon a solution, you may act immediately or do more research—talk with others, get advice, check out the data, and tweak or change some aspects, but you predominantly rely upon your own judgment, intuition, and what makes sense. Often inductive thinkers see the illogic and reject the common wisdom or tremendous trends of others—i.e., the Internet bubble in 2000. Some were highly critical of Buffett for his investment strategy of not going along with the herd during the tech-boom years.

Step 3

Finalize the internal decision based upon original internal thinking which may or may not be influenced by outside sources.

DEDUCTION

Step 1

Find out what everyone is doing. Read and research trends that influence your decision-making, and find out what the general consensus is before going to your own thinking.

STEP 2

Your own internal thinking now is influenced by the general consensus. That gives you confidence to make a decision, but it may be faulty if only limited or tainted data are available.

STEP 3

Finalize the decision based on original external thinking that is heavily influenced by outside sources.

Here are some examples of faulty thinking with bad results when leaders used deductive instead of inductive thinking:

In business: The Internet boom followed by the dot-com bubble of the late 1990s was labeled "irrational exuberance." Enron's model of growth to drive stock prices up resulted in faulty decision-making and resultant unethical behavior.

In sports: Teams do this when they see a team with a successful season and then copy the style without taking into consideration the personnel of their own team. For example, if a team adopts the style of another team that won the national championship using the "west-coast offense" without matching that offense to its own available talent, it may not work. This "copycat syndrome," often seen in sports teams, usually fails.

INDUCTION (BREAKTHROUGH THINKING)

| 1. Start inside with one's own specific knowledge. | 2. Go outside for the general, prevalent knowledge. | 3. Go back inside to finalize original decision usually with only slight or no modifications. |

DEDUCTION (INCREMENTAL THINKING)

| 1. Start outside with general knowledge available. | 2. Go inside to confirm or deny knowledge available. | 3. Go back outside to finalize decision. |

The analytical or integrative thinking personality trait involves knowledge, wisdom, judgment, and inductive thinking more than just raw intellectual skills. Leaders with inductive-thinking skills and syllogistic minds are able to start with their own internal ideas first, make decisions, then go outside only to see how others view a decision. From the great ancient military warriors of Sun Tzu and Alexander the Great to today's military and corporate leaders, we learn much about how to best apply the important analytical trait in its role of building modern teams. The era of working hard and winning is giving way to an emphasis on also working and thinking smart!

Working smart also requires a new way of communicating, beyond being articulate or even charismatic. We'll look at that in the next chapter.

Chapter 6

DYNASTIC LEADERS ARE COMMUNICATIVE

Watch your thoughts, for they become words. Choose your words,
for they become actions. Understand your actions, for they become
habits. Study your habits, for they become your character. Develop
your character, for it becomes your destiny. —*Anonymous*

Ideas matter and words matter. Both our ideas and our words endure for a long time and become our "brand," the lasting image people have of us.

EXAMPLES OF GREAT COMMUNICATORS

John F. Kennedy—"Ask not what your country can do for you—ask what you can do for your country."

Ronald Reagan—"Mr. Gorbachev, tear down this wall."

Martin Luther King Jr.—"I have a dream" (I highly recommend reading, Dr. King's "Letter from Birmingham Jail").

Barack Obama—"We are the change that we seek."

The word *communication* comes from the Latin *communicare*, which means "to share, to impart by giving or receiving". The importance of this leadership trait seems to grow daily as the style and ways we communicate often dictate our success or failure as leaders of teams. What people want most is to know what is going on, to be included, to have hope so they can predict what will happen with their life and thereby ease their worries and stresses. They want psychological well-being!

This chapter explores the importance of high EQ (emotional quotient), which leads to great communication, and the importance of having positive self-talks, and how to give and receive criticism.

IMPORTANCE OF CHARISMA

Research and experience shows that charisma is an extremely helpful trait to have as a leader, but *not a necessary* trait to be successful.

Many great leaders—political, military, business, and religious—have dedicated followers and tremendous accomplishments but are not themselves charismatic. But the research also shows that initial communication impressions are often more lasting than we previously thought, and leaders are often selected for this increasingly important trait. If one lacks it, other traits such as caring and honesty can make up for it, but one still needs to effectively communicate to the team.

Charisma will get you in the door, but it is not enough to keep you there!

POLITICAL TEAMS

Some people believe that Barack Obama won the 2008 election because of his gifted speaking skills, his relationship with the press, and his team's use of technology to communicate. Cell phones, the Internet, and new communication technologies are changing the world as we know it, particularly in less developed nations, and the leader who is deficient in using these skills will be less successful.

Obama is adept at using body language, narrative techniques such as storytelling, and phrase repetition (anaphora). Here's part of one of his speeches: "Tonight, if you feel the same energy I do, the same urgency I do, the same passion I do, the same hopefulness I do—if we do what we must do, then I have no doubt that all across the country . . . the people will rise up in November." It would appear that Dr. King was a major influence in his life, at least in the way he communicates.

Thinker—Rahm Emanuel, former chief of staff to Obama, Chicago mayor, and perhaps the second most powerful person during the Obama administration, was a veteran of the media-management business from the days of the Clinton administration to the present. He thinks like a journalist; his energy and charisma orchestrated the critical coverage of the White House. Some have labeled him "Hothead of State" and one psychologist identified him as "hypo manic" (low mania), with "a brain like a Porsche with no brakes and known for his foul language and explosive behavior, but his charismatic behavior was effective, at least with the media" (Gartner, 2009).

Coordinators—Secretary of Defense Robert Gates and Secretary of State Hillary Clinton, along with their own sub-team, have represented the Obama administration's people at the top.

FINANCE TEAM

» *Promoter*—Timothy Geithner, treasury secretary

» *Thinker*—Ben Bernanke, Federal Reserve chairman

» *Coordinator*—Lawrence Summers, former economic advisor

TEAM OF RIVALS

The effectiveness of this financial team will take years to determine both their short-term financial crisis resolution and their long-term economic stability-without-high-inflation success. What is most notable is the clear identification of the Promoter—Thinker—Coordinator team approach repeatedly in politics, business, or sports teams, although I am sure it is almost never viewed in this manner, or at least we are seldom consciously aware of the "team of rivals" approach necessary in building a successful group for enduring success.

Another great communicator, Muhammad Ali, has been dubbed "The Mouth," along with being a three-time world heavyweight boxing champion, Olympic gold medalist, and was voted "Sportsman of the Century" by *Sports Illustrated* and "Sports Personality of the Century" by the British Broadcasting Company. Many would say he was one of the greatest athletes ever, but almost all would agree that he was perhaps the best communicator in the history of athletics, and he said so—"I am the greatest." The man who gave us the sayings "Float like a butterfly, sting like a bee" and "A man who views the world the same at fifty as he did at twenty has wasted thirty years of his life" offered us much about how to interact with the press and communicate with others. (More about his insightful communication style can be found in Thomas Hauser's *Muhammad Ali: His Life and Times.*

Ali was sneaky smart. Blessed with an exceptionally high emotional quotient, he touched people all over the world. He could offend, but he more often charmed his followers like no other champion, who would chant his name: "Ali, Ali, Ali."

He is one of the most recognized names in sports history, right next to Babe Ruth. He was awarded the Spirit of America Award recognizing him as the most recognized American in the world in the 1990s. He received the prestigious Presidential Medal of Freedom in 2005. He was perhaps the best pure Promoter ever, with Angelo Dundee, his ever-present manager as his Thinker, and his longtime friend, trainer, and cornerman Drew Bundini Brown as his Coordinator.

CHAMPIONSHIP COMMUNICATION

The best cabinets in the history of the presidency have been those of George Washington, Abraham Lincoln (see the excellent Pulitzer Prize–winning book by Doris Goodwin, *Team of Rivals: The Political Genius of Abraham Lincoln*) and Harry Truman—each not afraid to surround himself with people who are accomplished yet who did not always agree, but could come together to be a winning dynasty. This is something the Carter administration lacked.

Having worked with Mrs. Carter on her mental health and caregiver projects, I was deeply touched by her compassion and caring, as well as her husband's. With an academic background in nuclear engineering, Jimmy Carter was overly analytical and even micromanaging while sometimes lacking the communication skills he and his staff needed to impact the media. At the Rosalynn Carter Institute for Caregiving in Georgia, Mr. and Mrs. Carter advise others on the matter they now prefer to communicate about: professional and family caregiving.

To help change national behavior and perceptions about issues in caregiving, the Carters embed journalists as interns at their institute, realizing that the journalists' future reporting work will benefit from this unique exposure to caregivers, special populations, and the support services they rely on.

My wife and I were fortunate to have a private session with Mrs. Carter, and she shared with us the need to change perceptions about people through the media by educating journalists about segments of our society that are often misunderstood.

EMOTIONAL INTELLIGENCE

Brilliant strategy and tactics have always been necessary for all great leaders of championship dynasties. But equally and even more important today in this instantly interconnected world, people skills and specifically communication skills are also essential. It's what you do and how you communicate your actions that drives your followers.

TEAM-TO-DYNASTY TIP #17. "The single most important ingredient in the formula for success is knowing how to get along with people." —Theodore Roosevelt

The *Harvard Business Review* has repeatedly noted in its special editions on leadership that the single biggest change in effective leadership in the last twenty years has been in the new emphasis on "people skills." The term "emotional quotient" was coined in 1995 by the psychologist Daniel Goleman and later refined with his colleagues. Research by various academic centers on more than a million individuals indicates we have moved away from the emphasis on IQ to EQ as the critical predictor of leadership success. Research now clearly shows that, in today's world, EQ is three times more important than IQ, which used to be the best predictor of leadership success until the 1970s. Additional recent findings indicate that the trajectory continues to push the emotional skills even higher for the future.

It has been my observation that getting along with people definitely entails knowing how to communicate well with them, as well as giving and receiving praise and criticism.

Yale psychologist Robert Sternberg, the most prominent expert on intelligence, states, "If IQ rules, it is only because we let it. And when we let it rule, we choose a bad master." Our emotions translate what we think about to what we feel, believe in and live every day. The Latin phrase for emotion is *motus anima*, meaning literally "the spirit that moves us."

Leaders with high EQ (emotional quotient):

» are in touch with their feelings.

» feel good about themselves.

» are fairly successful in realizing their potential.

» understand the way others feel and are generally successful in relating to people.

» are good at managing stress and rarely lose control.

A person with a high EQ can communicate with others in a variety of ways and with sensitivity and insight.

EMOTIONAL QUOTIENT EVALUATIONS

There are three main research centers that have published EQ assessments. Industrial psychologists Travis Bradberry and Jean Greaves founded TalentSmart. Robert Cooper and Ayman Sawaf, also psychologists, have coproduced the EQ Map at their Advanced Intelligence Technologies. Reuvon Bar-On, the most impressive researcher in this growing field, developed the most widely used tool, the Bar-On Emotional Quotient Inventory, which I have used successfully with thousands of CEOs and coaches. I have developed extensive databases that match the profiles of CEOs, coaches and professional athletes with each other and with the normal population and thousands of private patients who I have also tested. I find measuring a person's EQ to be the most beneficial and predictive of all the available tests today to determine leaders' ability to know themselves and their ability to connect with others across settings. I have used the Bar-On EQ Inventory at the NFL Scouting Combine for draft evaluations and in my national center for coaches. From NASCAR to all the major sports, it is by far the best guide to both individual and team performance.

The main categories of the Bar-On EQ Inventory are:

- » *Intrapersonal*—Self Esteem & Emotional Awareness
- » *Interpersonal*—Empathy & Interaction with Others
- » *Adaptability*—Flexibility & Problem Solving
- » *Stress management*—Stress Control & Impulsiveness
- » *General mood*—Optimism & Happiness

In working at the NFL Combine for the Miami Dolphins, I noticed other teams using antiquated and even questionable evaluation tools with poor results. Over the course of three days I had to evaluate the top eighty prospects that a team might use as a pool to draft seven individuals. I often had only half an hour to an hour to nail the evaluation. You can't be wrong when millions of dollars are riding on an evaluation, as well as the future of an entire organization. Coaches always tell you that at the college and pro levels winning is at least 50 percent mental. Personality traits and character are crucial to team chemistry. Those with high EQ scores performed the best and played the longest. I have found EQ to be the best predictor of performance on a consistent basis.

KNOW YOURSELF

In Latin, "know yourself" is "*nosce te ipsum*." As Sun Tzu said, "Know yourself and know your enemy." The problem for centuries, however, has been an over-focus on others and not on oneself.

In my consulting practice, I have found that leaders of championship teams or those who want to have a winning organization and eventual dynasty have one main barrier to overcome. It's what psychologists call "negative self-talks." It impacts our thought process and significantly impacts our EQ.

For example, one of the main negative self-talk strategies is called "filtering." That's where we take out all of the "good" and focus only on the "bad." One may get lots of positive comments, only to brush them off and magnify the few negative thoughts. This is common among perfectionists and people who are sensitive or caring. It is frequently found among the top coaches, athletes, and CEOs I have worked with. There are many more "negative self-talks" that require a cognitive-behavioral therapy approach to "knock out" the negativity and keep that winning edge (Stein & Book, 2000).

For example, if you slap the wall at two hundred miles per hour at a NASCAR track and scream obscenities at yourself for making a mistake, you can lose focus and get lapped or even wreck again. Or you can say to yourself, "No big deal; we will straighten the fenders out during our next pit stop and get back to the front since we have a fast car."

All of us every day are confronted with challenges, disappointments, and even criticism. It comes down to how we react to things in our mind— we can let things get to us or we can brush them off and move on. It is not easy but it's necessary for success.

GIVING AND RECEIVING CRITICISM

"What we've got here is failure to communicate," the prison warden said to an uncooperative Paul Newman in the classic movie *Cool Hand Luke*.

People want and need feedback! They want to know, "How can I get better?" Many team leaders, however, are reluctant to give or receive criticism. Some are too nice, can't handle conflict, or don't want to hurt someone's feelings or put up with the pushback—fearing a legal response. People dread annual reviews and tend to push people along with vague evaluations, or worse yet, skip them altogether. It impacts the process labeled SPEED—that is, Select, Plan, Execute, Educate, Document—but particularly the last of the six steps: data measures upon which to make decisions on individuals.

Giving and receiving criticism is a must—and there are ways to make it effective and painless.

GIVING CRITICISM

» Don't do it to prove you are right, blame others, or show your authority.

» Do it to make a positive change and help someone perform better.

» Don't jump around in your conversation—stay focused.

» Always use the "sandwich approach": Good—Bad—Good. This involves:

  * Praising the other person for his or her positive attributes in your opening encounter.

  * Asking questions about what went wrong and why. Often when given time, others will identify their own mistakes.

  * Ending with positive encouragement so that everyone walks away as if it was a "win-win" situation.

RECEIVING CRITICISM

» Welcome feedback—it can improve performance.

» Listen without being defensive.

» View it as an attempt to fix an issue rather than as a personal attack.

» Focus on solutions and problem-solving without blame.

» When you get hurt by someone, remember that there are usually four stages one goes through:

* *Hurt*—feel betrayed or like a victim

* *Anger*—get emotional and want revenge for being wronged

* *Healing*—begin to see why it happened and understand the reasons surrounding it

* *Forgiveness*—move on and reconcile or accept where the other person is coming from

COMMUNICATION STYLES

Each person is unique and has a style of communication (none is necessarily better than any other) based on his or her past and personality. It is best to know your own style from among the three distinct types identified with the type of leader you are—Promoter, Thinker, or Coordinator. You may fit nicely into one of the types or bleed over into others depending on how you view yourself. The main thing is that, in order to be a great leader, you must be aware of your own style and the styles of those you interact with.

THE PROMOTER STYLE OF COMMUNICATION

» Likes close personal relationships.

» Has the ability to gain support from others.

» Makes spontaneous actions and decisions.

» Likes involvement.

» Dislikes being alone.

» Tends to dream and gets others caught up in his or her dreams.

» Seeks esteem and acknowledgment.

» Has good persuasive skills.

» Is relationship-oriented.

» Is a risk-taker.

» Wants excitement and change.

» Enjoys the spotlight.

THE THINKER STYLE OF COMMUNICATION

» Makes cautious actions and decisions.

» Likes organization and structure.

» Asks many questions about specific details.

» Prefers an objective, task-oriented, intellectual work environment.

» Wants to be right, so can be overly reliant on data collection.

» Works slowly and precisely alone

» Has good problem-solving skills.

» Is task-oriented.

» Wants to be accurate.

» Enjoys solitary, intellectual work.

THE COORDINATOR STYLE OF COMMUNICATION

» Makes decisive actions and decisions.

» Likes control, dislikes inaction.

» Prefers maximum freedom to manage himself or herself and others.

» Cool, independent, and competitive.

» Has a low tolerance for feelings, attitudes, and advice of others.

» Works quickly and impressively alone.

» Has good administrative skills.

» Is task-oriented.

» Wants to be in charge.

» Gets results through others.

» Makes decisions quickly.

THE NEW COMMUNICATION SKILLS: IMPLICATIONS FOR TEAMS THAT WANT TO BECOME DYNASTIC

After consulting with hundreds of business leaders and sports coaches, I am constantly amazed at three phenomena. Number one is team leadership. I often hear corporate CEOs and coaches complain about poor leadership and I think—and occasionally say, if they are open to me—whose fault is that?

It's yours. You have not prepared your staff or players over the years to assume that role. You've gone on as if it is going to happen naturally.

As I describe in more detail in the later chapter on training, I believe in establishing intensive training programs that I label Leadership Academies for Corporations. The results have been dramatic; the programs prepare leaders at all levels so that communication and management are not always top down.

In sports, you may naturally have great leaders, but more often than not, if you do have great leaders, they tend to be quiet and keep to themselves and try to lead by being role models. This approach doesn't work that well. That is why I helped develop the concept of the "unity council" so successfully used at the pro and college levels, specifically in the University of Nebraska–Lincoln football program during the 1990s. (See chapter 8 for a more in-depth analysis.) It was a weekly process in which I met with seventeen players, elected by their peers, teaching them to lead as well as giving them a voice on how to manage the team. The peer pressure is powerful and it works. More than two dozen national collegiate and pro teams have adopted this "unity council" model, which within a few years, saw the 2007 New York Giants winning the Super Bowl after implementing a similar program for their teams.

The second phenomenon is the naiveté of coaches applying for head coaching positions. They show up for interviews so unprepared! Often their presentation involves, "Hey! Do you know who I am? I was a star player, have done great things, and you should hire me because I can motivate and I will win for you!" They naively fail to prepare a business plan or portfolio detailing their ability to recruit or draft, coach, fill seats, market, raise money, etc., etc. They don't realize they are the main PR voice and face for a university or franchise that will bring millions of dollars to its school, team, or community and that the selection committee—big or small—will be looking for a CEO as much or more as they are for charismatic coaches. If you want to be a coach, do your homework! Prepare a forty- to fifty-page plan that impresses people and shows them that you are uniquely qualified. It has been my experience that most coaches will reach the "finalist" level when they submit a detailed plan, and they are often selected unless politics takes over. But a great business plan at least gets you in the door and often the top job with the kind of respect one needs during early tenure. Perhaps this is the biggest reason for the massive turnover in coaches every four and a half years and CEOs every three and a half years. Corporations, big and small, from Fortune 500 to small start-ups, want a vision, a plan of how to get to that championship level.

The third phenomenon is poor communication skills, particularly when it comes to relationships, both personal and professional. On a personal level, the long hours can consume a coach or leader, with a major impact on his or her marriage and family. Coaches are supposed to be tough, and few witnessed open affection growing up, particularly those sons and daughters of parents who experienced the hard times of war, depression, and recession. But this is all changing, along with being able to relate better to others. Nothing turns players or employees off more, in my experience, than coaches and leaders who can't relate or connect with them. The best (Tom Osborne) was able to connect intellectually, physically (with a gentle tap on the shoulder and an occasional hug), and at a deep level, spiritually, by connecting in a special and unique way with each student-athlete or employee, no matter whether the star quarterback, a walk-on who never played a down, or the housekeeping staff. All were special to him.

TEAM-TO-DYNASTY TIP #18. The key to being a great leader or coach is the ability to treat your team equally, but each individual differently based on his or her unique personality. (We all love our children the same, yet treat them differently based on their personality.)

BUFFETT'S COMMUNICATION SKILLS

In 2003, before a game pitting Nebraska against Texas A&M, I accompanied Warren and his good friends Walter Scott Jr. and David Sokol on a pregame tour of our Nebraska football program. Following the tour, Warren delivered an inspiring pep talk to our Husker team. The players were glued to their seats as he asked them to imagine that he was going to buy each one of them a brand new car. "I would buy you any car you desire—Rolls, Lamborghini, etc." The student-athletes were buying into Warren's mind-boggling proposal when he added, "There is just one catch. The condition is, it will be the only car you will own for the rest of your life." Then he explained his analogy: "The car is a parallel to your body. You must take care of it—give it the best fuel, keep it protected, don't abuse it—because it is the only one you will have for the rest of your life." The players can recite, years later, that motivating message. And, yes, they won big! And, no, they did not get new cars!

Warren Buffett's ability to communicate with individuals at all levels of the investment world has likewise significantly contributed to his reputation as the greatest financial genius ever.

Whatever the era, the endeavor, or the end goal, the sine qua non is communication if a dynasty is to be built.

Well, there you have it. If you want to win in life, you cannot have a "failure to communicate." Welcome this trait, embrace it, and develop it as a critical skill, as it will only become more important in our connected world.

The leaders at the top and the roles they play along with their personality traits, six of which have been covered thus far, conclude this first section. The remaining three traits and the Process and Purpose building blocks for a dynasty follow.

CASE STUDY: THE RISE AND FALL OF A SPORTS DYNASTY

True business dealings of corporations, governments, and large organizations often fly under the radar away from public scrutiny. It is difficult to obtain confidential information.

Sports teams, however, receive plenty of media coverage and almost everyone seems to have some knowledge and loads of opinions. Sports are a type of international language spoken by many people and used often either to motivate us to imitate them and thus be successful—or to avoid the mistakes a team makes if it fails to win.

To illustrate, I chose two college sports teams I am quite familiar with. Examining football at Nebraska and Oklahoma, fierce rivals for many years, illustrates the dynamics of going from a winning team and even a decade-long dynasty in the sport to a losing program, then back to winning again. My behind-the-scenes familiarity with the programs perhaps puts me in a position to witness destructive actions and practices during the "selfish times" that bring down a dynasty.

These teams are worthy of studying to gain understanding of how they reached the championship level and stayed dominant for the final forty years of the twentieth century. What happened? How did the most dominant collegiate teams in America stay at the top for so long? And what caused their downfalls?

Insecurities, greed, arrogance, and most of all poor communication and refusing to understand and adapt to change within their cultures are key ingredients in explaining how these two nationally prominent college teams witnessed the rise and fall of their championship teams over a few decades. Below is an analysis of these two teams.

UNIVERSITY OF OKLAHOMA VS. UNIVERSITY OF NEBRASKA	
OKLAHOMA	NEBRASKA
Dominated in the 1980s—5 conference championships. Declined in the 1990s—0 conference championships. Reemerged in the 2000s—6 conference championships.	Dominated in the 1990s—8 conference championships. Declined in the 2000s—0 conference championships. May emerge in the 2010s.
Legendary coach—Barry Switzer's record (157–29–4) 83.7% coaching record and 3 national championships.	Legendary coach—Tom Osborne's record (255–49–3) 83.3% coaching record and 3 national championships.
Replaced in 1989 by Gary Gibbs—fired after 8–3 season in 1994.	Replaced in 1998 by Frank Solich—fired after 9–3 season in 2003.
New coaches resulted in a losing record over the next four years with embarrassing 60-point losses.	Head coach and AD fired after four years—first losing seasons in 40 years and embarrassing 70-point losses.
New athletic director Joe Castiglione, hired in 1998, hired Bob Stoops in 1999 and has immediate success, 109–24 in 11 seasons, 1 national championship and 3 runner-ups.	New AD Tom Osborne hired in 2007 hired B. Pelini in 2008 and immediate success, 9–4, 10–4 and 10–4 seasons.

THE FALL AND RISE OF OKLAHOMA

The top leadership during the fall and rise of Oklahoma:

FALL:

>> *Head Coach*—Howard Schnellenberger, 1995, & John Blake, 1996–98

>> *Athletic Director*—Steve Owens, August 1996–March 1998

>> *University President*—David Boren, 1994–Present

RISE:

>> *Head Coach*—Bob Stoops, 1999–Present

>> *Athletic Director*—Joe Castiglione, 1998–Present

>> *University President*—David Boren, 1994–Present

The president, AD, and coach all were replaced in 1994 after embarrassing behaviors by athletes under Coach Barry Switzer, only to have three different coaches follow him until Stoops was hired by the outstanding top AD in the country, Joe Castiglione. The program immediately turned around after the athletic department staff were let go, and Castiglione created a winning culture.

THE RISE AND FALL OF NEBRASKA

The top leadership during Nebraska's glory days:

>> *Head Coach*—Tom Osborne, 1973–97

>> *Athletic Director*—Bob Devaney, 1967–93 (Emeritus until 1996)

>> *School Chancellor*—Woody Varner, 1970–77 (CEO, University Foundation, 1977–87)

The downfall of Nebraska's athletic program was brought about by a perfect storm of failed leadership that dismantled the dynasty built by Devaney and others in the 1990s. From top administration officials through head coaches, the damage was rampant, and the program fell to shambles.

At the department level, a culture of mistrust and poor communication overtook the athletic program like a virus.

Portraits of old coaches were removed from the athletic offices; popular coaches and staff were replaced with mediocre, nonthreatening staff who were connected to the new leadership; contact with the media and boosters was tightly controlled and limited. Arrogantly, department leadership made clear that all statements and new hires would explicitly support the new regime.

Even as controls tightened, distrust took hold of department management. Some staff members, including me, were offered rewards in exchange for "snitching," supplying the leadership with inside information on staff and players.

Several prospective coaches turned down offers from the university as news of the dysfunction spread.

Nebraska's dominance in football just a few short years before was replaced with losing seasons and missed bowl game appearances. The failure of department leadership to support strong, effective coaches and honor the history and methods of the dynasty teams resulted in what a leading local sports writer called a "toxic waste pit"—a strong statement from the typically cautious Omaha press.

As the storm brewed in the department, the football program suffered on a micro level as well. Under new leadership, practice routines were changed to resemble those of pro teams, decreasing the intensity and discipline that sculpted the dynasty teams so successfully. The popular walk-on program that served the dynasty teams was abandoned. Former players and donors were alienated, leaving little legacy support for the team. Perhaps most embarrassingly, the coaching staff was subjected to public, profanity-laced tirades.

To top it off, the new leadership openly criticized former coach Osborne, further breaking the tie to the Nebraska dynasty that current players should have aspired to emulate.

What took forty years to build into a national powerhouse was destroyed in a mere four years.

As evidence of the damage, the team lost to Kansas (Kansas!) for only the second time in thirty-nine years. With a final score of 76–39, it was the worst defeat in the program's 117-year history.

Poor communication, a lack of empathy, and total disrespect for the dynasty that preceded it were the fatal flaws of the new football leadership. A leader who cannot create an atmosphere of openness and trust in his organization will not last, nor will his organization if he is in a leadership role too long. Firings followed the acts of disaster, but the damage lingered.

As the athletic program saw failures in top positions in the mid-2000s, university administration did nothing to combat the decay. Popular coaches were removed with the chancellor's support; celebrations such as appreciation dinners for former coaches were opposed and even sometimes forbidden; arrogant disregard for the responsibility of leading the school was obvious in public statements. More poor communication and lack of respect from the highest levels of leadership.

Though infecting the organization with distrust and disrespect is bad enough, there were financial consequences of such arrogance as well. An abrupt firing in the athletic department cost the university millions in a contract pay out.

Toxic cultures like that of Nebraska from 2003 to 2008 cause incalculable damage to morale. Although I personally was not treated poorly by the organization, I will never forget my home visits to talk with crying spouses and children whose husbands or fathers had been fired. Ironically, most were hired back some four years later.

Yet, where was the courage within the organization to speak out about the mistakes of leadership? Shame on all of us. One must speak out so that changes can be made and unethical practices not repeated. Many former players ask if I could do something. The administration wouldn't listen. That's why I left.

More of us should follow the advice of the famous monk Thomas Merton, who in his book *Seeds of Contemplation* wrote, "If a writer is so cautious that he never writes anything that can be criticized, he will never write anything that can be read. If you want to help other people, you have got to make up your mind to write things that some men will condemn."

There will be those who criticize you for speaking out. But if you care, as I did with six graduate degrees in our family from Nebraska, you must make sure that this type of abuse is not repeated.

The tragic downfall of the Nebraska program never needed to happen.

The athletic director was abruptly fired after his own staff turned on him and he left as the most disliked person in the state based on polls after having two losing seasons and missing bowl games for the first time in forty years.

———

Failures of sports teams, companies, and other entities are predominantly due to bad judgment and poor attitudes in leaders at the top. Oklahoma and Nebraska are great examples of this unfortunate phenomenon. These case studies show how great and successful organizations can rapidly fail if parts of the dynasty formula are missing or mishandled.

The only positive aspect of such a failing is the opportunity for rebirth.

TEAM-TO-DYNASTY TIP #19. The best time to make a major cultural-team change is when there has been a crisis or failure. People are more open to trying something new.

BUILDING A DYNASTY: PROCESS AND PURPOSE

While section I focused on the model—the People (Who) and their Personality Traits (What), this section examines the Process (How) and the Purpose (Why) of leaders guiding their organizations from teams to dynasties.

The observations and discussions I have had with leading CEOs, coaches, and military, church, and community leaders at all levels led me to formulate a five-step process which can provide aspiring leaders with a road map to follow.

The SPEED process—select, plan, execute, educate, document—has never been pulled together in this format, mainly because so many leaders are primarily tasked with only one piece of this chain. For example, if you are in human resources, your focus is on the selection step; those in operations focus on planning, executing actions, and measuring progress. This silo mentality brings about little interaction between these core process areas.

Timing is everything. It is another critical element in assuring a dynasty status. If the period or timing is off, it can be overcome with superior leadership and effort, but it will take longer and will be much more difficult. The process of building a team into a dynasty is accelerated when the concept of Timing (Period) and Culture (Context) are taken into consideration at each of the five steps, discussed in detail in chapter 7.

I had the opportunity to test this principle of timing and the right context a number of years ago in a Big XII basketball game. I had been team psychologist with the Nebraska basketball team for more than a dozen years. We had the greatest run in the history of the school during this time, with record NCAA appearances and a Big 8 conference tournament championship along with a national championship in the National Invitational Tournament.

It was always a scramble and difficult to win on the road. We were playing at Baylor, a school that had a good but not great team. Yet we had to win to keep our chances alive for a post-season bid! The timing of the game at this point in the season was critical.

I came up with a way to take the crowd out of the game—a huge advantage to home teams.

It had just been announced that Kevin Steele was to become Baylor's new head football coach. Kevin had been a linebackers coach at Nebraska a few years earlier and he was a good friend of mine.

So I went to our director of basketball operations, who helped me convince our head basketball coach, Danny Nee, to play a little psychological trick on the Baylor team and home crowd.

We had T-shirts in Baylor's green made up with "Congratulations, Coach Steele" printed on the front and "Head Football Coach" on the back.

During the one-hour warm-up and pregame "shoot around" the crowd was getting on us pretty good and the student section was cranked up for us. Nebraska was a big rival because of our football reputation. We went back into the locker room where the players all put on the T-shirts and proceeded to wear them during the entire fifteen-minute period of warm-up drills. Then just before we started the game, we had the players take the T-shirts off and throw them into the crowd.

It worked spectacularly! The crowd had the wind sucked out of them. We heard people say, "Wow! That's a class act." We were no longer the bad guys. Coach Steele came into our locker room after the game to congratulate us on our big win!

To many, it might appear that the best leaders—with character traits and a winning process to follow—would be enough to complete the championship formula. But there is one last building block—far deeper than the others—that serves as a foundation for the other three. It completes the formula and answers the ultimate question of *why* we lead.

I am constantly amazed at the number of people who make it to the top and develop awesome teams and even dynasties, only to have a colossal failure. It is not a new phenomenon. Kingdoms, empires, countries, wealth, and souls have been lost due to that deepest of all human essence—our purpose in life. "Know thyself" is so fundamental, yet so elusive for many. It's hard to believe how so many, who worked so hard, for so long, could throw it all dramatically away in such a short period of time.

Perhaps some can't deal with success, or the temptations that go with it. The mighty do fall unless they know themselves and seek a dream and a love to guide them and share with them the guidance of their mentor.

Success requires a great deal of energy and the adherence to rules to live by, which will be addressed in this book's final chapter. Next, though, the discussion turns to SPEED and how its five elements drive organizations to long-lasting success.

Chapter 7

THE PROCESS OF BUILDING A DYNASTY

If we take people as they are, we make them worse. If we treat them
as if they were what they ought to be, we help them to become what
they are capable of becoming. —Johann Wolfgang von Goethe

Goethe, considered the greatest writer/philosopher of his time, raises a great point: how we treat people helps them reach their potential. It is the day-to-day process of establishing, building, and maintaining a winning organization that is a dynasty leader's greatest challenge.

A number of years ago, I was being interviewed by a head coach of a top sports team at a major university. When we finished with the interview and he agreed to hire me to work with his team, I told him, "Coach, it will be fun to work with your team." He looked me straight in the eye and immediately snapped back, "Jack, winning is fun."

I got the message.

I have recalled that conversation many times and lived it on the sidelines, in the pits at races, in hospital rooms, courtrooms, and boardrooms of businesses.

Winning is fun. It's exhilarating to win a national championship or celebrate a case won, a breakthrough in research, or an award as being selected as the best in class in the country.

If you have the right people with the right personality traits and your timing is exact, then what is left is the process by which grounded individuals lead their winning organization.

However, this process is hard to achieve. Why? I have worked with, read about, and observed prominent leaders of organizations in all types of fields who fail. They are nice guys and gals who don't want to hurt others, but they often select or inherit the wrong people and fail to monitor and heed the warning signs.

You want and need dynasty leaders to succeed.

P3—PROCESS:
HOW TO BUILD A DYNASTY

The "how" of building a winning team can be best attained via a five-step process in which the emphasis on each step may slightly vary from company or team, but all five components are recognized as critical to success. My inspiration for this part of the winning formula comes from blending an analysis of my own experiences with parts from David Sokol's book *Pleased, But Not Satisfied*, and from former CEO of Honeywell International, Larry Bossidy, and Harvard leadership guru Ram Charan's *Execution: The Discipline of Getting Things Done*.

HOW?

SELECT—Spend up to 40 percent of your time selecting the right people matched to the right job at the right time. A critical process in building a championship team.

PLAN—Develop a strategic business plan or game plan that everyone is aware of and that gives vision to the goals to be achieved.

EXECUTE—Pull the trigger! Execute and engage in active decision making. Too often, difficult decisions are avoided, delayed, or delegated, resulting in impaired team functioning.

EDUCATE—Train and develop staff in an ongoing incremental process to increase skills among all team members.

DOCUMENT—Identify the critical factors, listen to the data and feedback in determining progress and implementing changes in order to achieve your stated goals.

I have referenced parts of their processes, expanded and clarified them, and matched the formula against historical dynasties, current Fortune 500 companies, and successful sports teams to provide examples of how winning dynasties stay successful.

The really good leaders follow this five-step process formally via their HR, training departments, executive team, etc., or informally each day without always labeling it so. They seem to have an intuitive grasp of knowing how to run a winning team long enough to develop into a dynasty. This is where SPEED comes in; it's the *how* of dynasty building.

STEP 1: SELECT

Leaders, coaches, or heads of teams have as their most important job the selection of their people, which should never be totally delegated. Bossidy's success was traced to spending 40 percent of his time selecting—personally making calls—as he believes "the right people in the right jobs create a leadership gene pool that delivers strategy that can be executed." In his first three years at Allied Signal, he personally interviewed three hundred new MBAs.

It sounds a lot like Jim Collins's analogy of getting the right people on the bus, getting people off the bus, and most importantly getting people in the right seats. The bottom line here is that most companies don't do their homework on the selection process, and we are witnessing a significant shift away from the old tendencies of how we hire leaders.

Recently one of the largest placement firms, Heidrich & Struggles, has announced a significant shift away from this old model of interviewing and placing upper management because there have been so many "busts." This publicly traded company has taken such big hits that it is radically changing its model to more consulting and only a 50 percent emphasis on selection and placement. There is a fee structure that often emphasizes getting people placed without looking at the long-term success rate. Besides, research clearly demonstrates a 3-to-1 success ratio in hiring internal versus external candidates.

The assessment process is also limited by what can be legally asked now. Cutting-edge research indicates that "behavioral interviewing" is yielding the best results for long-term success. This process involves structured interview questions that focus on a respondent's behavior and pragmatic problem-solving ability. The canned approach of the past is easily faked by candidates. Video recording and simulation testing of running a team is a more elaborate and expensive process, used more for the top leaders. Companies, teams, and organizations can't be wrong. Too much is at stake!

Sports teams, for example, vary greatly in their assessment process of both staff and the selection of their players. At the collegiate level, I have been surprised by the number of problems of scholarship athletes that are sometimes buried by their high school coaches as they realize this could hurt their chances of having a Division I scholarship for one of their players. Also, keep in mind—as I witnessed dozens of times—some athletes have severe psychological problems (for example, bipolar and psychotic disorders) that do not begin to manifest until the early to mid-twenties. New research indicates that a staggering 40 percent of all college students exhibit psychological disorders (per the American Psychiatric Association Diagnostic Manual—DSM-IV, 1994).

Forty percent seems too high. However, when we consider that 25 percent of the population has a definable mental illness, we realize that the added stress of college increases this percentage due to depression, loneliness, homesickness, drugs, alcohol, gambling, and relationship issues.

I was at first surprised to find that, for the student-athletes I tested—across all sports—40 percent also tested positive for psychological issues.

Even more worrisome is the finding that suicide is the third leading cause of death among young adults fifteen to twenty-four years old (according to the Centers of Disease Control and Prevention). Eight percent make a suicide attempt and 17 percent seriously considered making an attempt in a given year. (Goldstein, et al., 2008).

At the pro levels, the process of psychological assessment has been significantly improved in the last fifteen years, both qualitatively and quantitatively, but it has been described as still "in the Dark Ages" by me and other psychologists (Babb, *Kansas City Star*, 2010). I was shocked to witness at the NFL Scouting Combine (where top college football players are assessed in Indianapolis prior to the draft), where I tested the top seventy-five players in the draft for a top NFL team, team consultants who misrepresented themselves on their credentials. Some conducted sham evaluations or used weird instruments and came up with strange recommendations on whom to draft and why. One guy called himself "Doc." Come to find out, he was not a doc, not a Ph.D., nor was he a psychologist, and worked at a very low level at a state prison. He should have known that false claims of professional status are misdemeanors in most states.

Winning teams build their organizations on the selection process. Sports teams, in particular pro teams, accomplish this through the draft. As I interviewed and tested the number-one draft pick in the NFL draft, who later signed a $20 million bonus, I was convinced he was not even a top ten pick because of his "character" issues. The pro team I worked for did not take him and his career was far short of his unbelievable physical talent. His on-the-field talent never matched his off-the-field mouth, and character issues plagued his entire shortened career.

Another high-profile NFL team that had won Super Bowls used its pick, a top ten selection (the most critical pick in building a championship organization) to select a player I had worked a great deal with.

I offered to come in and meet with him and the new coaching staff to assist in his off-the-field personal problems. I was describing his background and how to best coach him when the head of scouting started mumbling, "You are killing me, man." I asked what he meant and he admitted that they had not done their homework on this athlete and therefore were not prepared for him during his first year in the pros, which was disappointing. He should have been the number-one pick overall, but he lasted only three years in the NFL. All the scouts told me he was the best talent in the entire draft, someone who at this level should last ten years, be all-pro, and become a Hall of Fame player. Not a bust!

His character issues and personality traits kept him from reaching his potential. The new coach of the pro team thought he could mentor him.

Contrast this with Bill Polian, the brilliant manager of the Carolina Panthers at the time, who flew in with eight members of his staff to our school. He interviewed the entire coaching staff, including me, and had a plan in place if they were able to draft this extraordinary athlete and football player. They had mentors lined up and incentives to motivate him and really impressed me with their preparation. They eventually bypassed him at selection time, concerned about his behavior.

All the major proteams now do at least some evaluations. One of my former basketball players, who was over seven feet and was drafted by the Seattle Sonics in the first round as the thirteenth pick, shared with me that his "tryout" with them consisted not of a single workout but a three-hour "psychological testing" by a highly qualified clinical psychologist. He was shocked, but it's a multimillion-dollar investment and they cannot afford to be wrong.

The importance of selection cannot be understated. Everyone needs to conduct due diligence by getting talented staff or players with character or you will eventually pay the price. It is often hard to get rid of mediocre staff, the bottom 10 percent that Jack Welch recommends cutting each year. It is disruptive and also very expensive—three to five times their annual salary.

STEP 2: PLAN

A good strategic plan is a set of directions for an organization. As Yogi Berra said, "If you don't know where you are going, you will end up somewhere else." It's a road map, penciled in so that changes can be made based upon the action needed to be successful. While most businesses are mandated to have detailed strategic plans, other teams, particularly sports teams, often have only a marketing plan at best—how to sell seats! Coaches need to better develop a business plan each year and pay closer attention to its economic impact on their organization, as well as the economic impact on the university or the community. It is often huge; each NASCAR race brings in an average of $30 million to a community via hotels, restaurants, etc.

STEP 3: EXECUTE

"Pull the trigger!" These are often my words to CEOs and team leaders. They often don't want conflict or to hurt others' feelings or to have bad PR and lawsuits. It makes news fast! Politics and personality deficits are often central. Many get elevated to one notch too high—the "Peter Principle"— and struggle. I recommend that you follow General Patton's advice—"A good decision today is better that a great decision tomorrow." Action, even if it turns out not quite right, is better than inaction, which paralyzes so many organizations, as David Sokol has often told me.

Execution involves day-to-day decision making, big and small. Listen to others, infuse your decisions with wisdom, and then move on.

I am not afraid of tomorrow, for I have seen yesterday and I love today.
—William Allen White

STEP 4: EDUCATE

It is also essential today to have an active training program—from orientation to ongoing development of staff. Academic training often fails to prepare individuals for the real-life crises and challenges they are faced with that can define success or failure. One individual on a team can have one bad day and cost the team its entire reputation and chances at a championship. Also, training programs need to be established to address the doubling of knowledge every five years, along with shifting demographics and demands on one's team.

Education and training programs can be powerful tools to enhance productivity, build unity, and promote cultural changes. You can shape behavior and attitudes and provide motivational incentives with properly designed educational activities.

STEP 5: DOCUMENT

Teams are measured by wins and losses and companies by quarterly returns. But it's the metrics that give you guidance. You have to drive your organization based on the data. "In God we trust but in data we decide," as a CEO friend of mine used to say. Sarbanes-Oxley legislation and Dodd-Frank regulatory requirements have dramatically altered corporate America with disclosure process and emphasis on "transparency." The NCAA and pro team sanctioning bodies also require an enormous emphasis on documentation to enforce eligibility rules. Teams that succeed in becoming dynasties carefully measure all these metrics that contribute to both successes and losses. As Jim Collins has stated, "Great companies also know what not to do."

Documentation is your blueprint to building a dynasty. Have you selected or retained talented team members? Do you have a strategic plan to follow? Have you properly executed your leadership duties? And is your educational/training program sharpening the skills of your team?

Your documentation process should answer these questions on a daily, quarterly, and annual basis.

───────

Some organizations have followed a slightly different process. Rather than this five-step process, some companies use what is labeled the 5P Process—an emphasis on product, philosophy, process, people, and performance expectations. The similarity to the S.P.E.E.D. process is obvious, of course: The point is, it's best to have a defined, structured process to follow in leading a team to dynasty status.

PAY ATTENTION TO TIMING

Never follow a legend! Just ask Jeffrey Immelt, CEO of General Electric, about timing and how hard it is to follow the legendary Jack Welch. GE, which is ranked by *Forbes* as the world's largest company, with 325,000 employees, and the fourth-most recognized brand, has had a very challenging decade.

When the decision was made in 2000 for Welch to retire and Immelt to take his place, GE's stock price was $60. Immelt officially took control on September 7, 2001—four days before the terrorist attacks on the United States. GE lost $600 million in insurance claims on that day. During the decade between 2000 and 2010, GE's stock price dropped as low as

$10 and had recovered to $20 at Jeff's tenth anniversary—two-thirds less than when he took over and 30 percent below the comparison benchmark stock market. Ouch!

Yet when you analyze the timing and context of timing for GE, from 9/11 to the greatest financial crisis in eighty years, Immelt has done remarkably well. The company's stock is on its way back and GE has been nimble enough to reinvent itself for strong growth in the next decade.

Timing and the context of timing are everything. Know when to get in and know when to get out!

THE BERKSHIRE HATHAWAY PROCESS

Berkshire Hathaway owns all or part of some ninety companies. The process he utilizes is primarily focused on the S—Selection—part of the SPEED process. He attributes his success to selecting the management of a company and allows its management to run it without interference. He prefers to offer guidance when called upon or will get involved if and when there is a crisis. He allows the company's managers to best determine their own strategic plan and metrics to measure their success. Yet in each company, whether he has all or part-ownership, one can see the Berkshire culture interwoven into the corporate behavior of the companies in which Berkshire is the largest stakeholder, such as Coca-Cola, *The Washington Post*, and Wells Fargo. The relationships are very personal, but in the end it is always about business.

CASE STUDY: NEBRASKA—TIMING

The Nebraska program hit a bottom in 1990. We were 9–3 that season and lost badly to Georgia Tech in the Citrus Bowl. Most programs would think that was success. But we were at a crisis—the team was no longer highly ranked and there was lots of national criticism. The exact moment of change came at halftime of the Georgia Tech game. Tom Osborne gave an emotional speech about his health and how he thought just a month earlier it might be his last game. Although his health improved, he said you should never take anything for granted. He had tears in his eyes. Just then, our all-American defensive lineman, Kenny Walker, who was severely hearing-impaired, read his lips and got up and gave the coach a huge bear hug. Our middle linebacker saw this and pounded the Gatorade table and drinks went flying everywhere. The team went crazy. They deeply loved their leader and were very touched, as was I, at how deeply he cared about them and the message he wanted to share about leadership. We played three times better the second half but were too far behind to win. As a result of that loss, however, Coach realized changes needed to be made.

That off-season, Osborne made some major changes. He never went on a vacation. He demanded that his staff recruit better (Selection), change the defense to a 4–3 from a 5–2 alignment (Plan), supported my work with the players to better perform, such as presenting pregame psych-up videos (Execute), allowed me to implement the Unity Council (Educate), and for the first time ever evaluated every assistant coach and held everyone in the entire program more accountable (Document). The result was the best recruiting class ever—a 60–3 record and the highest number ever of players from Nebraska being drafted in the NFL. He inspired every-one—from coaches to equipment managers—to perform at their very best, every single day.

PAY ATTENTION TO THE CULTURE
AND CONTEXT OF TIMING

Knowing the culture of your team and adjusting your style of leadership often determines your success and the speed of your success.

Obviously, if a company had had twenty quarters of prosperous growth, increased stock dividends, market share increases, and high morale, any decrease or break will be viewed as a failure. Even though market trends are cyclical and may be negative for an entire industry, the leaders at the top will always be held accountable. The buck stops with them. That's why you are paid the big bucks, they are told.

Similarly, successful teams may face unrealistic expectations, as did UCLA after Wooden and Nebraska after Osborne. Of course, the opposite is also true. Quick turnarounds from poorly performing teams will give their leaders more credit than perhaps they deserve.

Unfortunately, your dream job may open up only once in a lifetime, and if the timing is poor for your skill set and personality, it still may be hard to turn down—even knowing your odds for success are low because you may not get another shot at it.

Every CEO, head coach, and leader I have interviewed strongly agrees that the period of time in service as leader plays an essential role in ensuring long-term success. Unreasonably high expectations can be overcome, given time—even if it was the right thing at the wrong time—but it is twice as hard.

The success of Blue Cross as a health-care model can be attributed to timing, as Anderson deduced from his original sociological research. Eighty-plus years ago the country was simply ready for it, and now it is embedded into our culture so deeply it will last for hundreds of years. Odin W. Anderson, author of *Blue Cross Since 1929*, made a profound discovery: "If the concept is sound and the leadership adequate, the movement is on its way."

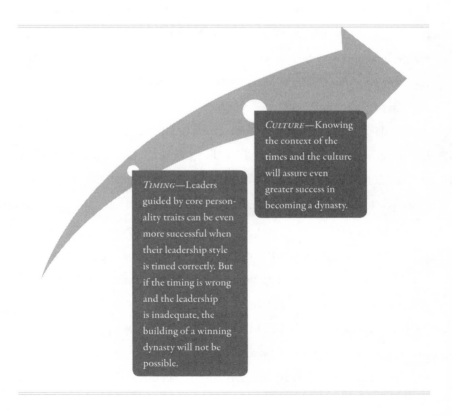

CULTURE—Knowing the context of the times and the culture will assure even greater success in becoming a dynasty.

TIMING—Leaders guided by core personality traits can be even more successful when their leadership style is timed correctly. But if the timing is wrong and the leadership is inadequate, the building of a winning dynasty will not be possible.

If the concept is unsound, behind the times, or to far ahead of its time, any leadership could fail. According to Anderson, if the concept is an expression of an idea "whose time has come, it will succeed even under barely adequate leadership, and it will succeed brilliantly under brilliant leadership."

Some of the most profound ideas are often old ideas, long forgotten and buried in obscure places. When brought together with additional carefully selected findings, they can make for a powerful winning formula.

IMPACT OF TIMING AND CULTURAL CONTEXT

» What type of leader do you want?

» What type of leader is needed now?

» Who is making the selection?

» What do you want that leader to do?

The culture and context you inherit needs to be carefully analyzed to ensure success. If you are a military leader, is it a time of peace or a time of war? If you follow a coach with a boring style of play, are you a good fit? Does a corporation need a marketing or branding guru after suffering the loss of market share under a previously brilliant CEO?

Historical context, or what is called "contextual intelligence," is an important factor. This involves knowing your team culture as well as its political, social, technological, and demographic contexts.

TEAM-TO-DYNASTY TIP #20. Timing and context are everything. Know when to get in and know when to get out! Life is timing. As that Kenny Rogers song goes, "You got to know when to hold 'em, know when to fold 'em."

A more specific breakdown of this "how" of leadership involving the five-step process follows in the next two chapters. A greater emphasis on the selection process is presented first because if you select the right people for the right positions at the right time, so many problems are avoided, and it dramatically accelerates the speed of moving your team to the status of dynasty.

Chapter 8

THE PLAYERS IN YOUR DYNASTY

Never doubt that a small group of thoughtful citizens can change the world.
Indeed, it is the only thing that ever has. —Margaret Mead

Imagine for a moment that you are the leader of the Baltimore Ravens.

You want to apply this championship formula to build your team into a dynasty—to win multiple Super Bowls and dominate the NFL for a decade.

You have a head coach (Thinker), the general manager (Coordinator), and the owner (Promoter)—the people at the top. They exude the character personality traits. Now you want to implement the first step of the process to build your team: selecting the best players.

The general consensus is that you recruit the best players via the draft. You very carefully select the players who will bring you that trophy.

Preceding the draft is the NFL Scouting Combine, where invited players perform physical and psychological tests. My responsibility was to recommend the top players from a mental/psychological perspective.

Working for the Miami Dolphins, I used a three-part examination with each of the prospects as we meet one-on-one in hour-long sessions. The instruments I used are: the Mental Performance Index (MPI), the same as the profiles I present in this chapter, the Emotional Quotient Inventory (EQ-i), and a biographical analysis via interviews.

So there I was, sitting across from one of the top players in the 1996 draft. I will never forget this young man from the University of Miami. His name was Ray Lewis. The consensus of all of us on the Dolphins evaluation team, including the coaches, general manager, and scouts, was "Wow! We want you on our team."

Of all the players we evaluated, Ray impressed us most. He showed us a passion for being the best. Having grown up in a tough neighborhood, he had challenges to overcome. He was also a bit undersized, and some teams thought he was too small to play the linebacker position. Those teams blew it!

The Baltimore Ravens drafted him in the first round.

He is a twelve-time Pro Bowler who has played 16 years in the league, is the heart and soul of the team in leadership, and may go into the Hall of Fame as one of the very best players ever at his position.

The Baltimore Ravens needed more players like him. They have been a good team, a championship team—but just short of a dynasty. That's what selection does—that's how critical it is to an organization.

Selecting the right players, matching them to the best position and continually motivating and providing feedback to improve behavior will maximize your chances of having a winning organization.

MATCHING PEOPLE TO POSITIONS: CORPORATIONS

Too many companies and teams have been burned by a selection process in which candidates smooth-talk their way through the interviews. They are savvy on how to beat the system. To counter these disappointing results, more companies are using better selection techniques and some are even conducting very expensive and elaborate video analysis and simulation of crisis-management situations to see how effectively the candidate makes decisions.

I have listed the following selection instruments for you to use and adapt as you select and evaluate your players in corporate *and* sports settings.

BEHAVIORAL ASSESSMENT

Most of the instruments used today fail to be valid—particularly in the predictive validity areas—because future behaviors depend on so many variables.

The cost is another factor, as the best tests, though standardized on thousands of subjects, can be conducted only by licensed clinical psychologists in each particular state. The availability of these qualified individuals only adds to the cost factor.

The best tool available today is the behavioral assessment process. It is a structured, objective analysis process designed to pinpoint the select behaviors you feel are critical to a job. It uses the principles of behavioral analysis of leadership behavior to design what I have labeled the Behavioral Assessment and Selection Survey (BASS). I researched and designed this test myself. It is a powerful tool that I have successfully used with numerous Fortune 500 companies to select—for hiring or promotion—the best and brightest.

This survey is presented in Appendix B to show you how you can adapt and apply it to build your own dynastic team.

I (1) explain the purpose and use of the survey; (2) present a selection of the top ten behaviors for a particular job; (3) define behavior; (4) develop probing questions for each leadership behavior; and (5) share a scoring chart to grade a candidate for comparison.

360° EVALUATION

Over 85 percent of major corporations today use some form of 360° evaluation. Feedback from all those individuals who interact with you at all levels can be a powerful tool if used correctly.

I recommend designing your own 360° evaluation rather than using an expensive customized design or an off-the-shelf version, which may miss the point and be overkill. Keep it simple. Ask three questions: (1) What are the strengths? (2) What can this person do to get better? and (3) What can the entire team do to get better?

You want to increase the frequency of positive behaviors and focus on how to improve them rather than on eliminating the negative behaviors, because most people know what these are and don't know how to get better.

MATCHING ATHLETES TO POSITIONS

Psychological research has identified the eight behavioral factors that best predict athletic performance. If you want to have players who can take you to the next level—dynasty level—focus on evaluating each of the eight athletic performance factors listed here.

ATHLETIC PERFORMANCE FACTORS

» *Confidence*—High self-concept and self-esteem. Assurance of one's own abilities.

» *Coachability*—Understanding and responding to instruction. Attentive and willing to follow direction.

» *Self-motivation*—An intrinsic desire to prepare and compete at a high level all of the time. An enjoyment of the sport.

» *Competitiveness*—An inclination to compete, a sense of rivalry and aggression, and a strong need for victory at all cost.

» *Work ethic/persistence*—An understanding of the importance of practice and dedication. An ability to continue to prepare and perform through all situations.

» *Team player*—Each player has an obligation to the team as a whole. An understanding of the necessity of team cohesiveness.

» *Concentration*—Ability to focus. Ability to learn and retain material—cognitive skills.

» *Mental stability*—Emotional balance. Ability to avoid drugs, alcohol, and mental health problems.

REJECTION PROFILE

After talking with scouts for pro teams and observing the selection process, I identified the following behaviors as "red flags." Teams who may reject candidates based on these behaviors or, at a minimum, require much more probing an investigation.

10 REJECTION PROFILES

» *Addiction*—drugs, alcohol, gambling.

» *Criminal behavior*—legal problems.

» *Paranoia*—mistrusts others, hard to coach or get along with.

» *Anger*—has difficulty controlling emotions, is impulsive, argumentative, physically or verbally abusive.

» *Depression*—severe depression, moody, withdrawn, avoidant.

» *Immaturity*—doesn't fit in or get along with others, nervous, hyper, gets too psyched out.

» *Personality disorder*—lies, cheats, manipulates, is selfish, doesn't fit in.

» *Laziness*—noncompetitive, no mental toughness, won't work hard or prepare mentally.

» *Emotional concerns*—severe emotional problems, spacey, "out of it" at times, has been dangerous.

» *Learning problem*—inability to focus, attention problems, comprehension concerns.

MENTAL PERFORMANCE INDEX

I learned a great deal about the critical process of evaluating leadership potential while working at the NFL Scouting Combine in Indianapolis. I had to evaluate the top one hundred athletes for the draft, and I had less than one hour each with very little background information on which to base my report.

I had to be spot-on, as the wrong decision could cost millions. Remember the draft where the Colts took the number one, Peyton Manning—now a Hall of Fame QB and one of the best ever after fifteen years—over the number-two pick in Ryan Leaf, who lasted only a few years in the NFL and was a bust? Many analysts predicted that Leaf was stronger, with a more powerful arm, and would have a better career than Manning. Look at what happened to these two picks and their respective teams with this single decision. Manning took the Colts to championships—a dynasty—and the Chargers struggled for years to just be a good team.

I developed the Mental Performance Index (MPI; see p. 164) and used it with the Dolphins. It reveals high draft picks who will perform well on the field, but as I accurately predict, will struggle at times off the field.

I developed this index and you can develop your own similar index by following the steps to compare candidates and predict who will best fit in your organization.

I identified the top thirteen behaviors the team looked for in an athlete. The most important seven were scored on a 1 to 10 scale and the other six were scored on a 1 to 5 scale, since they were less important factors.

I asked probing questions, took a careful history, and utilized portions of the Emotional Quotient test to evaluate and rank each athlete for the team's draft decisions.

The circles in the table represent how this one candidate, a high first-round pick, scored. He had a good career, but not a great career, and the MPI was spot-on even after fifteen years of seeing how successful he was.

MENTAL PERFORMANCE INDEX (MPI)

Name _____ Position _Running Back_____

School _____

Date _____ Evaluator _Jack Stark_____

ENERGY LEVEL	2	4	6	8	(10)
MENTAL CONFIDENCE	2	4	6	(8)	10
COMPETITIVENESS	2	4	6	(8)	10
RESPONSIBILITY	2	4	(6)	8	10
WORK ETHIC	2	4	6	(8)	10
AGGRESSIVENESS	2	4	6	8	10
ATTITUDE	2	4	6	8	(10)
GOALS	1	2	3	4	(5)
PERSISTENCE	1	2	3	4	(5)
CONFIDENCE	1	2	3	(4)	5
SELF-STARTER	1	2	3	(4)	5
STABILILTY	1	2	(3)	4	5
FACES CONFLICT	1	2	(3)	4	5

THE IMPORTANCE OF TEAM UNITY

When I first started with the Nebraska team in 1989, we had a star player and team leader who was a good guy but who came from a tough background and was intent on making it in the pros (which he did). He told me, "Nobody helped me; why should I help others?" He was really a good guy, but he was just being honest and looking out for his own interests because he had "no home to go to." I knew we needed to change this attitude. So after the failed 9–3 season in 1990, after my second year, and having gained some credibility, I went to coach and suggested the concept of a "Unity Council." Coach Osborne asked me what it was and if it would work. I told him, "It will work pretty well the first, second, and third years and by the fourth or fifth, we could win a national championship." I thought that was bold and that he would be ecstatic. He wasn't! He told me that I "did not understand—that this was football and we had to win and win right now!" I had never seen him so animated. I got the message and instantly doubled my time with the program.

The Unity Council consisted of seventeen players: eight offense, eight defense, and one kicker. (I loved my kickers, but one was enough!) The position representatives were elected by their peers. We met weekly throughout the year—just the players and me. It was a vehicle for players to address and deal with player concerns and behaviors—class attendance, attitude, players getting into trouble, etc. It was a smashing success. Why? Not me; I only coordinated the meetings and reported their concerns confidentially back to Coach. Tom, being a psychologist, understood the importance of peer support and letting the players feel that they had a voice in the program—and they did. We changed things and adjusted.

The players held each other accountable and generated dozens of stories in which players helped each other, and cared about each other. It produced the greatest five-year run in college football in the last fifty years. The power of caring, which permeated the entire program, was evident in the posting in the meeting and locker rooms with big signs that read "UNITY."

Holding each other accountable and focusing on this one thing—unity—changed the entire culture of the team. In 1991 and 1992, we got much better and then took off for five straight seasons. It takes time to change the culture of an organization. But if the formula is in place, the results are stunning.

Here are Coach Osborne's comments on the Unity Council excerpted from his book *Faith in the Game* (chapter 7, "Unity," page 110).

"To say that the Unity council was solely responsible for improved performance is too simplistic. There is no question, however, that it contributed to an improved attitude, which, in turn, translated into success on the field.

"After the Unity Council was initiated, we won seven consecutive conference or divisional titles and three national championships. I am convinced that exceptional team chemistry was a key factor in this stretch, and that the Unity Council played a significant part in developing this chemistry."

THE 5% DIFFERENCE

When I started with Nebraska in 1989, I told Coach Osborne that I could make only a 5 percent difference—thinking naively that that was minor.

He looked at me and said, "Jack, are you kidding? Five percent at this level is huge! That is the difference between a good team and national championship team." Boy, was he right. In the 1980s we won 82.5 percent of our games. In the 1990s we won 88.5 percent of our games and 95 percent of our games during the last five years Tom coached.

TEAM-TO-DYNASTY TIP #21. The difference of 5 percent in winning or ROI can be the difference between a mediocre and a national championship team.

HONORABLE MENTION TEAMS

» New York Giants

» Indianapolis Colts

» New England Patriots

» Pittsburgh Steelers

Two pro teams and dozens of college teams (e.g., Missouri, Florida State, and LSU) have used the Unity Council concept with similar success.

The New York Giants' sixty-four-year-old coach, Tom Coughlin, winner of the 2008 Super Bowl, was almost fired after the 8–8 2007 season. Fans wanted him fired—so he changed. He established an "advisory committee" of veteran players and participated in off-the-field activities. Borrowing from the Unity Council format, players saw a different side of him. His star player, Michael Strahan, said, "He became a totally different coach. Without that change, I don't think we'd be here. I don't think you would get the same response from players he's gotten." (*USA Today*, June 19, 2008, p. 7c.)

» *Promoter*—Eli Manning—Super Bowl MVP

» *Thinker*—Tom Coughlin—Giants head coach

» *Coordinator*—Jerry Reese—Giants general manager

The Indianapolis Colts were winners of the 2007 Super Bowl and runners-up in 2010. Tony Dungy is one of only two guys to win a Super Bowl as both a player and a coach. One of the most dominant teams in the NFL in the last decade, the Colts team is headed by one of the most impressive leadership trios in all of sports.

Promoter, Peyton Manning. The time I spent with Peyton Manning revealed one of the most impressive pro athletes I have ever met. Obviously, he comes from a great family, but his reputation as a man of character has to be at the very top among all athletes.

Thinker, Tony Dungy, 2007 Coach of the Year. What a man! His book *Quiet Strength: The Principles, Practices and Priorities of a Winning Life* is an inspiration to us all. He has overcome tragedy (the loss of his son) to become one of the most respected leaders in all of sports. He is very much like Tom Osborne—a classy, spiritually based leader both in and out of coaching.

Coordinator, Bill Polian, four-time General Manager of the Year. There is not a better mind and nicer guy in all of pro sports at his level. He is one of the top ten most impressive people I have met in my lifetime. I had the occasion to work with Bill at an NFL Scouting Combine, and I also attended many of his talks to numerous college teams. He took Buffalo to four Super Bowls and helped launch the Carolina Panthers in addition to his years with the Colts.

All of these men are the epitome of a caring or servant leader.

The New England Patriots were Super Bowl winners in 2002, 2004, and 2005. These championship teams developed into a dynasty during the 2002–2005 years, winning three Super Bowl titles in four years. Only Pittsburgh in 1975, 1976, 1979, and 1980, with four Super Bowls, San Francisco in 1982, 1985, 1989, and 1990, and Dallas in 1993, 1994, and 1996 have similar records as championship teams that became the dominant dynasties of their eras.

» *Promoter*—Tom Brady was Super Bowl MVP in 2002 and 2004

» *Thinker*—Bill Belichick

» *Coordinator*—Owner Bob Kraft

The Pittsburgh Steelers were Super Bowl winners in 1975, 1976, 1979, 1980, and 2009 and were runners-up in 2009.

» *Promoter*—Quarterbacks Terry Bradshaw (1970–83) and Ben Roethlisberger (2004–present)

» *Thinker*—Coaches Chuck Noll (1969–1992) and Mike Tomlin (2007–present)

» *Coordinator*—Owners, the Rooney family

Sports dynasties are national and international obsessions. They have their own language and culture. They are capable of teaching us much about leadership and team building in constructing long-term successful organizations. Perhaps because of the media coverage—you can't go inside the boardroom of Microsoft during a meeting—we know more about the dynamics of a sports organization and thus learn valuable leadership lessons.

The importance of a sports team to a state's psyche was brought home to me a number of years ago when a philanthropist and former CEO of a successful construction company, Walter Scott Jr., said, "There are three things we can't have next year in Nebraska—a drought, another recession, and a mediocre football record." Wow! I did not realize, with my being so close to the team, how important it was to the entire state for so many reasons.

Sports teams are not life, nor are they always the best metaphor for life, but they do provide valuable lessons on how to build either a team or successful business that lasts long enough and is so effective as to become a dynasty.

TEAM-TO-DYNASTY TIP #22. President Harry Truman wasn't afraid to have people around him who were more accomplished than he. That's one reason why he had the best cabinet of any president since George Washington.

SELECTING AND RETAINING MOTIVATED PEOPLE

"If you have family, friends, good health, and a reasonable amount of money to get by on, you have a very blessed life." This is the advice I received from a good friend many years ago.

With that thought in mind, I start each morning with a prayer.

I pray for our family and me to be healthy, happy, and successful!

That's the real definition of winning in life. I suspect that deep down inside this is what each of us wants.

But how do we do it? Why is winning so important, yet so elusive?

We read books, attend motivational sessions, receive training and work hard. But things simply don't change! Those who want to be better leaders are more discouraged than ever.

It is very difficult to find a management book that is even close to providing a new and fresh idea. Perhaps this is why people who want to become change agents turn to such unusual sources for leadership tips. Thunderbird pilots, Navy SEALS, pro-sports coaches, and motivational gurus offer books ranging from "this is how I did it" to fables.

What I hear so often is "There is really nothing new out in leadership, so what I do is pick up a few tips each month wherever I can."

It is as if we have a giant invisible backpack we carry around and as we come across a new leadership topic we throw it in the bag. This approach results in a hodgepodge of ideas scattered about with no unifying model or blueprint to follow.

A few years ago I attended an expensive dinner conference for two hundred top managers of large manufacturing company. The company was down to three thousand employees after peaking at six thousand. The new CEO wanted to make a splash and brought in a top motivational speaker at $65,000 for his half-hour presentation titled "Winning and Success." The presentation was entertaining but less than stirring.

Two weeks later I polled dozens of the "Winning and Success" attendees. Not one attendee could tell me a single thing the speaker had said, let alone how the speech changed his or her behavior.

What a waste of money, time, and talent! It even caused a backlash of resentment with the union because of the lavish spending.

The bottom line is changing behavior—motivating others to perform both ordinary and extraordinary tasks each day.

A number of years ago I was consulting to this same manufacturing plant. The CEO of the plant asked me to take charge of a project. For our next town hall meeting involving all the employees, he wanted to show a videotape sampling dozens of workers. The video showed me interviewing people on the floor. I asked a simple question—one that at first I thought was kind of dumb but that turned out to be incredibly insightful. The question was "What motivates you?" I was surprised at the answers. Not one person was negative. The answers all settled on the importance of being appreciated, working with colleagues they enjoyed, and the pride they took in their work. Not a single person mentioned money.

My takeaway from this experience is that most leaders don't know how or what motivates their staff.

Research findings below point out the discrepancies between what managers think their people want and what they really want.

At this same plant, the culture changed after three different buyouts and countless reorganizations and layoffs. When we tried to hire three hundred employees, more than a third were not able to be retrained; they flunked their background check, failed their drug test, or failed to show up after a few weeks.

WHAT DO EMPLOYEES WANT?		
Items rated by employees & employers	Rating by employees	Rating by management
1. Appreciation	1	8
2. Feeling "in" on things	2	10

3.	Help with personal problems	3	9
4.	Job security	4	2
5.	Good wages	5	1
6.	Interesting work	6	5
7.	Promotions	7	3
8.	Management loyalty to workers	8	6
9.	Good working conditions	9	4
10.	Tactful disciplining	10	7

The challenge is to find motivated workers. How? The chart below emphasizes the importance of "internally motivated" workers—individuals who have always been this way, because it is ingrained into their personalities. Be sure to select these top 25 percent rather than those who are only motivated externally ("What can I get?")—the bottom 25 percent.

I designed the following motivation chart to best explain this leadership attribute.

MOTIVATION

Internal	External	I & E (both)
25%	25%	50%
» Upbringing	» Money	» Pride in Job
» Responsibility	» Stock	» Craftmanship
» Self-Motivation	» Benefits	» Product Quality
» Work Ethic	» Training	» Satisfied Customers
» Family	» Paid Tuition	» Coworkers/Team
	» Respect & Recognition	

THE MOTIVATION PROCESS

In order to maximize the potential of staff members and retain them, a dynastic leader needs to understand the complex process of motivating player behavior.

It is a circular process where one's work behavior is dependent upon a number of variables, each interacting and building upon the other.

The behavior of team players is determined by (1) the products they produce, (2) how they are evaluated, (3) the supervision they receive, (4) how they are rewarded, and (5) where they are in their personal lives.

Understanding and mastering these variables adds to the speed of transforming a good team into a dynasty.

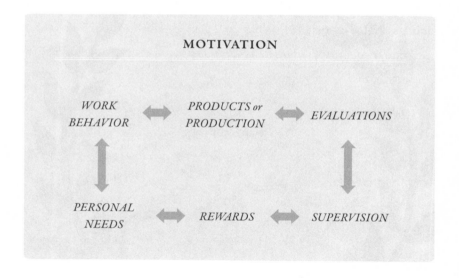

Chapter 9

PLAN—EXECUTE—
EDUCATE—DOCUMENT

You're better off backing a mediocre idea that's brilliantly implemented than a brilliant idea that's badly executed. —General Georges Doriot

Have a plan!

Have a really great plan that is fresh and flexible and anticipates all possible scenarios. The best leaders talk about being able to look around the corner to see things that others don't see.

This gift is exemplified in a psychological experiment that was titled "Inattentional Blindness." It was designed to teach us that we can miss obvious things in life that are all around us.

A YouTube hit, this video involved a basketball team dressed in black playing another team dressed in white. You are asked to count the number of passes the white team makes in thirty seconds. The answer is fifteen. But that is not the point. The psychologists wanted to demonstrate that we become so intent on counting the passes that 50 percent of viewers fail to notice this big gorilla that strolls onto the screen and beats his chest.

A visionary leader can tell you not only the correct number of passes, but also how many times the gorilla beats his chest. Attention to detail!

If you have the right players who can design a precise plan, then everything follows naturally in executing the plan, educating and training others around it, and documenting its effectiveness in order to tweak it as you go forward.

A number of years ago I had an opportunity to consult for a season with the Hall of Fame college basketball coach Eddie Sutton of Oklahoma State. His son Sean Sutton was in charge of the pregame scouting report.

Sean had played for his father and was a great player in his years at the school.

I had been fortunate to sit in on hundreds of pregame and halftime scouting reports by coaches over the years across many different sports. I was excited to sit in on the first report by this young assistant coach. His ability to design a plan of attack against the other team and to adjust at halftime was brilliant. I was in awe.

Sean's insight, analysis, and detailed anticipation were a real gift, something you rarely see; but then a coach's son often has it in his DNA.

Sean painted a picture by breaking down the opponent's offense and defense and the tendencies of each player of the opposing team.

You could feel the confidence of his team grow with each play as they anticipated everything thrown at them and in the end decisively beat a better team.

THE PLAN—DYNASTY LEADERS AS VISIONARIES

Caution! Many wannabe dynastic leaders confuse tactics with strategy, a recipe for disaster.

Why? The lack of vision—the ability to make decisions with an eye toward the big picture.

For example, after the 2011 earthquake and tsunami hit the Fukushima nuclear plant in Japan, my contacts in the nuclear industry shared with me that the real failure of the Japanese power company was its emphasis on tactics.

The plant's management engaged in "linear thinking," as do many great engineering-led organizations. Their thinking was, "First we do this—get water on the reactors—then reduce the chances of explosions; then we plug the radioactive water leak, then restore power and proceed with cleanup."

This is a slow, linear, methodical process. But a multiteam, multi-tasked, well-coordinated approach to tackle each of these challenges—simultaneously—would have been much more effective. Leaders need to be open to new ways of doing things, defining new strategies while making decisions with an eye toward the big picture.

The greatest "process" challenge or day-to-day task of building a team into a dynasty is communicating this plan as a vision of the future—who are we, where are we going, and how can we best get there—in such a way that it draws others in and speaks to what others feel and see.

Followers want visions of the future that reflect their own aspirations.

They want to know how their leaders got their vision and want to have input so everyone can get there together with total buy-in.

Few leaders, however, make a habit of working on this skill. Research shows that only 3 percent of the typical business leader's time is spent quietly envisioning and thoroughly developing a comprehensive strategic plan.

Being visionary is not the same as being charismatic. Visionary leaders answer the question of "where we are going" for everyone. No vision—no leadership.

EXECUTE

Decision-making can be an awesome responsibility. Leaders at the top have a profound impact on the livelihood and happiness of their team members. Perhaps this is why it is sometimes difficult to make the tough decisions.

When hit with a crisis or a defeat, dynasty leaders know how to re-group, reorganize, and live to fight another day.

"I wish I had acted sooner. I delayed the inevitable, hoping the num-bers would get better." That's what I often heard during the "lost decade" from business leaders.

In the end, delaying decisions does more damage when everyone is laid off, merged, or dismantled.

Another execution behavior I often see is the focus on short-term results. I was very fortunate in 1978 to have had lunch with my graduate school hero—Dr. B. F. Skinner of Harvard. Skinner ranks next to Freud in his impact on society in the past century. His theories on how human behavior is shaped through positive and negative reinforcement permeate the ranks of leadership teams all over the world. Skinner has also had a profound effect on the world today, evident in everything from marketing to economics and social programs.

He taught me two lessons, the first of which was patience—for what you write, do, or say today may take years to be fully appreciated.

I asked him if he was frustrated that although his groundbreaking book *Science and Human Behavior* was first published in 1953, people were just beginning to understand his work and all its applications.

His response surprised me. "No, I am not at all frustrated, Jack. Look at Einstein. His findings have taken us fifty years to understand and we still have not been able to totally understand all of it. It could be another fifty years."

The second Skinner lesson was his advice on the problems of human behavior. He said our biggest challenge is society's inability to delay gratification. Perhaps it is human nature that people lack patience while expecting immediate gratification.

Maybe this explains the "I want what I want and I want it now and I am entitled to it" behavior. Countries are in debt, we are using our natural resources faster than we can replace them, and our obesity rates climb worldwide.

EDUCATE

All great leaders of teams that become a dynasty are by definition great teachers and educators. Education is inherent concept of leadership, which implies guiding or imparting knowledge and thereby changing behavior. Hall of Fame athletes and world-class CEOs, to the person, can recite the teachers and mentors in their lives who had a powerful impact on their development. Those leaders whom I have encountered along the way who were good but not quite great seemed in almost every case to lack a mentor or teacher to fill a deficiency that has sadly held them back.

Teaching is a reciprocal behavior-changing process. I was fortunate enough to have directly taught or consulted in the classroom at the pre-school, middle school, high school, undergraduate, graduate, and medical residency levels. It taught me to both appreciate the great teachers (and I had many) that I had and to realize how difficult it really is on a day-to-day basis. It is life changing to see one's ability to impact other people's lives, which in turn hones one's own leadership skills. My fondest memories and best teaching were with middle school inner-city kids. You can really make a difference in young people's lives if you are a dedicated teacher.

The concept of the personality trait (P2) "teach" found in the nine C.H.A.R.A.C.T.E.R. traits is interconnected and reinforces the concept of "educate" found in the (P3) "process" steps of S.P.E.E.D.

Leaders teach every day through their actions, words, and decisions. Establishing formal and informal education or training programs is vital for the building and maintenance of a dynasty.

These educational efforts build skills, change behaviors, and shape the culture of an organization.

At the heart of Stephen Covey's book on *The Seven Habits of Highly Effective People* (1990) is the notion of continuous improvement—"sharpening the saw." It is not a new concept. The term *kaizen* (a combination of the Japanese *kai* = change and *zen* = good, or improvement) has been in use in Western business for the past fifty years. Toyota is a great example of its use, and *kaizen* is why it is the largest automotive company in the world today. This philosophy fuses the notion of continuous improvement in all areas of one's life—forever. When applied to work, individuals at all levels can participate in kaizen from the CEO down to all employees in their quest to always get better. This philosophy differs from the old command-and-control leadership style that has dominated organizations—both corporate and sports—since World War II. Those companies and teams that have embraced collaboration and emphasized teaching have survived at a much higher rate.

BUFFETT ON TEACHING

What a wonderful teacher! From his early days of earning extra money teaching at the Scarsdale Adult School to speaking at top economic conferences or weekly on CNBC appearances, Warren is a very talented teacher. One of his greatest but seldom talked about legacies in the last few years is that over twenty times a year he hosts large group of MBA students who spend the day with him. For example, my son was delighted to "ride shotgun" with Warren in his modest Cadillac as they drove to Warren's favorite Omaha steakhouse for lunch when he treated the group of over one hundred University of Chicago MBA students. Warren spent an entire morning with them sharing his wisdom in the form of stories, insights, investment philosophy, and his personal views on life. He thoughtfully answered all their questions. Then he took time to pose individually with each of them for a photo before treating the group to lunch. Warren joked with them, telling them not to embarrass him by ordering *foie gras*! My son loved it, and his classmates, after hearing hundreds of CEOs from all kinds of the top global companies in their coursework, indicated that it was the highlight of their entire MBA experience.

EXEMPLARY CORPORATE TEAMS

I have selected various exemplary corporate teams that have achieved world-class status because of their tremendous focus on training programs as well as championship sports teams particularly noted for their culture of teaching and mentoring athletes in improving their performance. GE and Procter & Gamble, along with PepsiCo, Cisco Systems, and Google, are recognized as the best incubators of talent and are prime targets for recruiters selecting CEOs to run businesses elsewhere. Their education programs are perhaps the single biggest reason for these companies' continuing to thrive.

THE GENERAL ELECTRIC TEAM

Much of the success of GE is due to its leadership model and its emphasis on developing talent through its internal training programs. These training programs spawned continuous leaders in the company by promoting internally, as well as dozens who left to become fantastically successful CEOs at other companies. They are perhaps what GE is best known for. General Electric's famed management-development center in Crotonville, New York, is a sprawling complex, complete with a luxury hotel and golf course. It has churned out hundreds of leaders trained in their various courses and seminars as GE acquired companies during the 1980s and 1990s. More recently, the company's emphasis has been on internal expansion rather than acquisitions as they launched the new training experience Leadership Innovation and Growth (LIG) for all senior business-management teams, consisting of a total of 175 individuals.

PROCTER & GAMBLE

P&G, founded in 1857, is the eighth-largest company by market cap, the fourteenth most profitable, and the tenth most admired company in America. It spends twice as much in marketing as any other company in the United States. At P&G, the CEO from 2000 until 2010 was A.G. Lefley. He increased sales 110 percent to $84 billion. Why was he so successful? He developed a rigorous training program called Build from Within. It tracks the performance of every manager, making sure each is ready for the next job. The top fifty jobs have already identified the next three replacement candidates. His replacement and former COO, Bob McDonald, indicates that by training and promoting internally, their leaders thrive (compared to the 50 percent failure rate of placement firms). This bench strength is critical to the success of the company, and research has proven it should be used by more teams.

TEAM-TO-DYNASTY TIP #23. One of the biggest challenges in molding and keeping a winning team is selecting and developing talented people. The key is to have a leadership training-and-development processes that change leaders' behavior and perpetuate winning.

INFOSYS

On a global scale, the best example of teaching is at Infosys Limited. Infosys is a global consulting and information technology services leader that has embarked on a journey to build the "foundation for any business institution that aspires to endure for generations." This very successful company in India is led by its chairman, N. R. Narayana Murthy at its 334-acre training institute at Mysore, Karnataka. He calls himself "chief mentor." He recognizes that the global demand for talent is growing more intense and that Western talent is shrinking. Infosys has become the best model (according to a Boston consulting group report) of how a global company meets today's demands by having an understanding of the talent it needs to execute its strategies and how to acquire, develop, and reward that talent.

In developed economies, companies often take fifteen years to develop a leader. In emerging countries, many companies are targeting a five-year path. This is being done by building leadership training teams of high potential recruits and experienced mentors to accelerate development via an in-house university system made up of hundreds of "faculty." Multiple training tracks are also offered to build managers.

Few companies are prepared for the looming talent shortage. In the USA, 75 million baby boomers are approaching retirement and only thirty million Generation X-ers are available to replace them.

In the European Union, the working-age population is forecast to fall by 48 million, or 16 percent by 2050.

Countries such as India, Brazil, and Russia, which have highly educated workers, can help fill this need. In China, there are 375 million students, twice that of the United States, in higher education between 2007–2015.

SMALL BUSINESSES TO SPORTS TEAMS
AT SMALL SCHOOLS

It is perhaps helpful to point out here that the same principles of people, personality, process, and purpose also apply to small and family-owned businesses and sports programs. This championship formula is possibly easier to identify with less bureaucracy and layers of leadership. You don't have to be a large organization to have this formula work.

Often, owners, coaches, and staff are required to also formally train and teach—it makes them better coaches and bosses. For example, the legendary John Gagliardi, head football coach for over fifty-five years at St. John's University in Collegeville, Minnesota, in his mid-eighties himself, has won four national titles. Another example is my involvement for the last twenty-five years at the University of Nebraska at Omaha with its former head wrestling coach Mike Denney (Promoter), who has won eight national championships, and, more important, dramatically changed the lives of thousands of young men both on and off the mat and in and out of the classroom. With the best chancellor in the school's history, Del Weber (Coordinator), and its grandfatherly athletic director, Don Leahy (Thinker), this three-person team took athletics to a national level. The same thing is happening at Creighton University, a small Jesuit university in Omaha, with the Promoter, head basketball coach Greg McDermott; the Thinker, athletic director Bruce Rasmussen; and the Coordinator, president, the Reverend Timothy Lannon, SJ.

There are many more isolated centers of excellence in which national championships are being won and family-owned businesses are thriving without vast sums of financing.

The most powerful way for leaders to communicate and motivate and change the culture of an organization, if needed, is to spend a significant portion of their time training their core team members the way Warren Buffett and Jack Welch did. Much of their success comes from this emphasis.

I have spent the major portion of my consultation time demonstrating this with big and small corporations and with sports teams at all levels. *Academy* is the title I assign to these educational programs, as that word best describes the learning that takes place. Each leadership academy's training is based on the organization needs of the company and moves the entire company towards our strategic goals.

The same principles apply to sports teams and the use of team meetings and the Unity Council, resulting in winning games and championships.

DOCUMENT THE DATA

Trust, but always verify!

This is the refrain I often heard from a friend who was an engineer and plant manager.

Metrics—measures of specific accomplishments—serve as a scorecard in guiding decision-making and the allocation of resources in all businesses today. They are crucial steps in building effective organizations.

In sports, teams have season and game goals, and the great coaches spend time reviewing progress each week—giving feedback on how to get better. There is often general theme—"Refuse to lose," "Unity," and "Unfinished business" were some of the mantras used by Nebraska football. It helped to identify what we needed to emphasize to build that winning culture.

In another example, the U.S. Army recently developed the Global Assessment Tool (GAT), a survey to identify the training needs of recruits in emotional, social, family, and spiritual fitness areas.

Annual reviews have become an essential process of corporations at all levels, yet most are dreaded and done poorly or fail to change the desired behavior. A few years ago, when the new CEO of Gillette took over, sales and profits had been flat for years. In looking at performance reviews, he found that 74 percent of the managers had been given the highest rating and only 3 percent had received the lowest. He quickly dumped the process. If you select or inherit "C" players with apathy, you can address their deficits via the educational process of the academy.

Today more than 80 percent of Fortune 500 companies utilize a form of 360° feedback. This fifteen-year-old concept involves getting feedback, often anonymously, from everyone around you—boss, peers, and direct reports—regarding your leadership skills. It can be more powerful than the traditional 1-to-5 point Likert scale, with 1 being very low and 5 being very high. The Likert is a psychometric scale commonly used in questionnaires. It is the most widely used scale in survey research. In these scales most people get a 2.5-to-3.3 score, which does not mean much. I design one for each specific team. I find the personal statements of strengths and areas of improvement by the 360° process to be the most powerful part of the evaluation and very effective at changing behavior. The use of scales 1 to 5 or 1 to 10 usually results in scores clustering in the middle, and many are indifferent to these scores. But specific personal comments cut to the core and get people's attention.

The documentation process completes the process of building and maintaining that championship formula.

Good teams that want to win championships or be the best in class require a process of these five steps of Select, Plan, Execute, Educate, and Document. It takes discipline and attention to detail to follow these steps, but the results make it worth it.

The next two chapters address the issue of purpose—why lead? I have observed burnout, boredom, self-sabotage, emotional issues, and a loss of passion that prevent a championship team that seems to have it all—strong leaders at the top, great character traits, superb processes—from achieving its potential as a dynasty. The missing element is often a lack of purpose.

Chapter 10

PURPOSE—
THE GUIDING FORCE

He who has a why *to live for can bear almost any* how.
—*Friedrich Nietzsche*

If you have a purpose or reason for living, you can deal with all of the difficulties life can present. I often tell leaders that this is not Heaven, it is earth, and on earth, there is a lot of pain and suffering. This is the central theme in the most remarkable book I have ever read.

When I was in college I read Victor Frankl's *Man's Search for Meaning* and it changed my life. First published more than fifty years ago, it has sold millions of copies and has influenced people all over the world. Frankl recounts his horrible experiences in the Auschwitz and Dachau prison camps during World War II. A prominent Jewish psychiatrist in Germany, Frankl was arrested along with his family and friends and shipped to the death camps. His "job" was to carry out dead bodies from the gas chamber. Knowing that most of his family and friends had perished, he struggled with the question "Why live?"

In the most horrible conditions in the history of mankind, he found a purpose—a *why* to live for: *I need to live to teach others the purpose of life.* His book details his experiences and how he developed a philosophy of living called "logotherapy"—the "therapy of meaning." He believed that if he could help people identify their purposes in life and why they want to live, he could help them overcome all obstacles.

P4—PURPOSE

All great team- and dynasty-building leaders need to address the "why" issue. What's my purpose—what gives me meaning in life? Our standards of living have dramatically increased, yet our levels of happiness and satisfaction are going down. Something is missing. It's not money. Research tells us that after the first $50,000 there is no correlation between money and happiness. In other words, after our basics are taken care of, our level of happiness is determined by the meaning we find in our lives.

WHY?
PURPOSE

A DREAM—Pursuing our passion and dreams in life gives purpose, meaning, and a reason for working hard to win in each of our lives.

A LOVE—Life is not complete without finding someone to share it with. Joy and happiness will surely follow when this occurs. Life is not an easy journey.

A MENTOR—Finding caring persons who can guide and direct us, particularly during our younger years, but also throughout our entire lives. Mentors will keep us on the path to winning in life.

There are three major schools of thought on what drives people. Freud believed it was the pursuit of pleasure. Alfred Adler believed it is the pursuit of power, particularly among leaders. And, as I just described, Victor Frankl believed it was the search for meaning in our lives.

The most compelling research on this subject in my lifetime comes from a former Yale psychologist named Daniel Levinson. In his book *The Seasons of a Man's Life*, written more than forty years ago, he analyzed the adult life development of forty male Harvard graduates over a sixty-year period. He found that a person is fulfilled by essentially three things: (1) a vocation or job that fulfills his or her dream of accomplishment; (2) a love or someone to share life with; and (3) a mentor or someone to guide him or her.

I have found this research to be of tremendous help, particularly with corporate and community leaders as well as coaches: It is not only lonely at the top; it is also very difficult to be successful. One poor decision out of a thousand and high-profile leaders can be trashed by the media. This research really resonates with these leaders, as it helps explain the essence of their personal satisfaction and happiness. If you have a great job, someone who loves you, and someone dedicated to teaching and mentoring you, you can deal with the loneliness and criticism that come with being a leader today. When you have these three things that give you a purpose, you can make it over a long period of time—the time it takes to build a dynasty. Many leaders can't maintain their behavior; they burn out, get off track, or lose their focus and drive without a purpose.

People often fail for psychological rather than intellectual reasons. I witnessed this phenomenon in consulting with top corporate leaders and coaches in my non profit organization, National Center for Coaches.

Depression, burnout, unhappy marriage, a terrible childhood, and a lack of someone who cares enough to be a mentor are a few underlying psychological challenges that interfere with sustained success and fulfillment of a dream. Leaders may be smart, with lots of skills, but if they lack a real purpose—a dream of what they want in life, a love to share life with, and a mentor to guide them, they won't last long

Mergers, acquisitions, reorganizations, layoffs, and firings, along with the disappearance of entire industries, has resulted in a significant decline in job satisfaction—less than half the population likes their job, and many blame their leaders.

I spent a lifetime treating patients with stress-related disorders. What shocked me most was the toll it took on leaders and workers alike. Heart disease, cancer, headaches, pain, sleep disorders, and GI ailments had an even bigger impact than depression and anxiety.

And what's most disturbing is that many leaders are either unaware of or trapped by the unrealistic expectations placed on them.

The result is a midlife crisis or irresponsible, even thrill-seeking behavior to counteract the pressure. The result: affairs, drinking, gambling, or drug abuse. It is as if they can't get off life's treadmill, so they unconsciously and impulsively do something stupid, resulting in being removed from their position. They could not walk away from the addictive job, so they were removed; that way it's not their fault, as someone else removed them (a board, a church, a university, etc.).

I developed a formula—"Happiness is a function of security and predictability." People are most happy when they are secure and can predict the future so they don't worry. This basic happiness formula can best be fulfilled when one has a championship formula to guide them.

A LOVE TO SHARE LIFE WITH

My father used to tell me, "It does not matter when you get a raise or a promotion if you come home and have no one to share it with."

Finding and keeping a love is more difficult than ever. Half of marriages end in divorce and in the other half, the level of marital satisfaction is challenged daily. I always make a central point of involving the spouse or significant other when consulting with a leader. The spouse or significant other is the person whom leaders spend the most time with, are often influenced by, and bounce ideas off of. These "partners" play a significant role in supporting the leader, and I like to involve them in this critical support system that is often woefully thin. Many leaders come home each night drained, as if they are a giant switchboard that everyone at work plugs into, and one way they get recharged is by those waiting for them at home—spouse, kids, and significant others who help refill their energy. And a small but growing population is choosing to not lead at all—to avoid jobs of responsibility—as it extracts a heavy toll on themselves and their families.

A MENTOR TO GUIDE YOU

Those leaders who struggle the most, I find, lack a mentor in their lives. It is getting more difficult to find people willing to mentor, people who care about another person and will spend the time to bump that person along the path of life. Many corporate mentoring programs have now been initiated without a lot of success, according to research, but mentors are critical for development, as we never outgrow our need for guidance.

Corporate mentorship programs were all the rage during the last decade. A human resources department's dream—another project they could introduce under their sponsorship. Unfortunately, the research showed that formal company-sponsored mentorship programs failed to accomplish their goals.

What we learned is this: It is hard to find good mentors. They often lack the time to invest; assigning someone is ineffective compared to a natural match based on authentic interest; the expectations that many mentees had—that the process would result in rapid promotions—were unrealistic.

Mentors can be found at all levels and don't have to be leaders, although this is often even more beneficial. A mentor should contain the personality traits (P2) of teacher and may be successful with the (P3) step of Educate in the more formal process found in training programs. While each of these three factors (mentor, teacher, educator) are different, there are some similarities and overlap. If you can be (mentor) and do (teach and educate), you will always be in demand.

The number one predictor I find in identifying who will make it as a pro athlete is that individual had or has a great mentor—a father, mother, coach, teacher, or minister—someone who cared enough to offer constructive criticism and make him or her a better person.

I have few regrets in life.

I regret perhaps only a few minor things I did along the way.

But what I most regret is what I did not do.

Two regrets hang over me most.

I am perhaps influenced in this way by the many individuals I was privileged to counsel during their last days. I found that what dying people regretted most in life was what they did not do. They regretted living their life for others, for not taking more risks, for never doing the things they dreamed about. Or for not spending more time with those they loved most.

The first regret arose at my best friend's funeral. Salt died of cancer at age fifty-three. Through high school, college, and graduate school we spent time together nearly every day. At his wedding at age twenty three, he weighed 130 pounds—down fifty pounds from his athletic level. He had been diagnosed with cancer and was not expected to live long. I was his best man. Over the course of his thirty-year marriage, I saw how his courage and love for his wife, Anne, helped him defy the odds of surviving his cancer for three decades. Salt spent his entire career in education and was an awe-inspiring teacher in the true meaning of "awesome." Yet it hit me at his funeral that I regretted not spending more time with him during our adult life. He was such a major influence during my formative years. In many ways he served as a peer-mentor to me.

He was successful because he had a dream (to teach others), a love (someone who loved him so deeply despite many who warned her that he would not live long), and lots of mentors along the way, while mentoring so many himself.

My second regret also arose at a funeral. Frank was my chief mentor in life. I wish I had spent more time learning from him as his life was drawing to an end. His mentoring gave me professional success during the first twenty years of my career. But more than that, his passions for justice, for the dignity of life, for teaching, for friendships, for art, and for his family gave me fresh perspectives, values, and insights. Frank was a highly principled and uncompromising man with exceptional character.

He could have earned more money and been promoted to higher levels if he had acted like so many "leaders" we see today who compromise or let money change their behavior. Instead, he spent his entire life working with and advocating for people few wanted to serve—those with "intellectual disabilities." In the process, he became the most decorated psychiatrist in the world for his contributions. I learned so much through his almost daily guidance. We wrote many books together. But I regret that I was "too busy." When he was near the end with cancer and he knew it, he said to me, "Let me teach you something." He was not finished with me and wanted to teach me more. I should have, as I look back, cancelled all my appointments and spent those "Tuesdays with Frank" moments as frequently as I could. He left me with great advice; I've listed some of his wisest insights below, as "Guidelines."

TEAM-TO-DYNASTY TIP #24. "To be kind to all, to like many and love a few, to be needed and wanted by those we love, is certainly the nearest we can come to happiness." —Mary Roberts Rinehart

---

Don't live with regrets. Spend as much time as you are able with your mentors and teachers.

GUIDELINES FROM FRANK MENOLASCINO, M.D.

» Always provide more service than what is required. Most people provide the minimum.

» Love what you do.

» Allow your opponents and others you deal with—especially your opponents—to have self-respect.

» Never expect a thank you—give them, and also be appreciative if you get them, but never expect them.

» Be patient. Use ten short passes to score a touchdown, not one long pass.

» Once you have made a decision—that is it. Do not fret over it. It was your decision, live by it, respect it, and go on to the next decision.

» The luckiest people I know work the hardest.

» Be happy and not afraid to express affection. It will make your work easier and more effective.

BUFFETT'S PURPOSE

For Buffett it was never about the money as much as it was about the challenge and the competition; money was just a way of keeping score. He perhaps inherited this dream of being successful from his mentors—his father, the politician, and Ben Graham, his professor at Columbia. Everyone needs a mentor, and he was fortunate to have had two great ones in his life, particularly early in his career to help guide him.

His love was his wife, Susie, a talented musician and mother of his three kids, whom he adored. They called her "big Susie" and his daughter "little Susie" or "little Sooz." Watching Warren with his daughter one evening was delightful! You can see she has so much admiration for him, and he is very proud of her—and rightfully so. She runs her own large foundation dedicated to educational causes. His older son, Howard, has a foundation that focuses on the agricultural aspects of world hunger, while his younger son, Peter, is a musician, artist, and author (*Life Is What You Make It*). Each of them gives to others in very meaningful ways, in keeping with their father's philosophy of giving his children "enough to do anything, but not enough to do nothing."

PURPOSE COMPLETES THE CHAMPIONSHIP FORMULA

Think of leadership as leading to a dynasty pyramid. At the top are the right people in their most productive roles. Next are the personality traits of these key leaders, followed by the processes of conducting one's leadership of the organization.

The base and foundation, however, involves one's purpose in life—something we rarely think about except perhaps when we are in a crisis. "Who am I? What do I want to be? Where am I going? And how can I best get there?"

Good questions to ask. The answers help to keep everything in perspective in both good and bad times.

Purpose impacts performance, which impacts winning. And winning impacts more winnings.

In my role as a performance psychologist, I am often called upon to help others perform at their peak level, from boardrooms to athletic contests. In order to assist others in performing their best, I have them think of a diamond-shaped mental preparation process broken into four levels: First, the last forty-eight hours; second, the last twelve hours; third, the last four hours; and fourth, the last hour. At each level, I have them go through a mental preparation process of getting them ready to perform at a specific event.

In NASCAR, for example, I have them focus on the technical aspects of the race—their car, the track, all strategic things—forty-eight hours before the race to improve practice times. Then, during the last twelve hours, I have them get organized (equipment, clothes), visualize, and finally relax just before they go out.

I often do hypnosis or deep relaxation with individual athletes in mixed martial arts or Olympic sports.

In football at Nebraska, we developed one of my favorite team activities, which I labeled the "psych-up video." I designed a six-to-seven-minute pre-game video for each game during that remarkable run of 60–3 over five years. Different players are featured in each of the videos showing off their unique styles of motivation, humor, and "psyching-up" their teammates. We complemented the players' cameos with highlight clips, music, and additional motivating footage. The psych-up videos could really get the guys fired up! Our team watched the videos during our pregame preparation just before we dressed. Then the locker room was quiet as each person began to mentally prepare himself.

The objective of these psych-up videos was to remind the players one last time of the purpose of their performance, which would help them perform their best. The videos were often dedicated to their mentors, who were helping them achieve their dream of winning a championship, also acknowledging the support of family, friends, fans, and, most important, each other. Our team unity was, we were told by many analysts throughout the country, the best they had ever seen in college sports.

The most memorable psych-up video was the night before the national championship bowl game against Peyton Manning's team in early 1998. I had recorded a message from selected seniors on the team who spoke about each of their positions' coaches and especially their head coach, Tom Osborne. The players talked about how special each coach was to their career and dedicated the game to them. There were few dry eyes as the video played. We beat a very talented team the next night by three touchdowns.

Conclusion: One's purpose in life, as described in this context, forms the basis of leadership success over a long period of time. The final two personality traits of Energy and Rules to Live By have been moved to the next and final chapter. These two traits augment and serve to reinforce the dream-love-mentor component, as it demands hard work and adherence to the various rules we all have to follow. These rules, found in civilizations, countries, communities, clubs, and churches and in every segment of society, when followed will bestow the "dynasty" status on any team.

Chapter 11

ENERGY & RULES
TO LIVE BY

*Your first and foremost job as a leader is to take charge of your own energy
and then to help orchestrate the energy of those around you.* —*Peter Drucker*

*Only work half a day. It doesn't matter which half you work—the first
twelve hours or the second twelve hours.* —*Kemmons Wilson*

The single greatest predictor of success for a leader and his or her team
over the last sixty years has been hard work. It is a legacy handed down by
that greatest generation, the one that saw us through WWII.

"Whatever you do, work hard," they told their kids and grandkids.

That advice worked and produced a booming world economy.

It all changed, however, during the financial meltdown of 2008–2010.
The rules have changed. It is still important to work hard, but everyone
now has to also work smart. How? What does that mean? More education used to guarantee a better lifestyle, but even this process is being
questioned.

The last two personality traits—Energy and Rules to Live By—are presented here, as they overlap and reinforce the process and purpose components in closing and wrapping all together this championship formula.

An illustration from General Colin Powell, retired four-star general and former secretary of state, relates to working hard and smart.

Powell recounts the story of when he was a young infantry officer at Fort Benning. There were a lot of old captains who had served in World War II and Korea. They really knew their soldiering. He learned a great deal from these reserve captains. He tells the story of a brand new second lieutenant who was very ambitious and wanted to be a general. One night at the officer's club the young officer spotted this old general sitting at the bar, and he went up and said, "How do I become a general?" The general answered, "Son, you've got to work like a dog." And the general went on to describe what that meant. "So is this how I become a general?" the young officer asked. "No," said the general, "that's how you become a first lieutenant, and then you keep doing it over and over." Throughout the careers of dynastic leaders you see that they did their best today, thought about tomorrow, and dreamed about the future. But doing your best in the present while working smarter by being more efficient is the best advice today.

ENERGY

Energy, which includes hard work, passion, and mental toughness, is essential for being a leader on a winning team. Leaders are made, not born, and it is not luck or accident, it is more like the cliché "the harder I work, the luckier I get." One is reminded of that old Ringo Starr song, "It Don't Come Easy."

The number-one bestseller in business books for a number of years was the brilliant book *Outliers: The Story of Success*, by Malcolm Gladwell. He has captured the secrets, he believes, to success and wealth. This book investigates why certain individuals are able to have such amazing careers, earn accolades, and win in so many areas of life.

Malcolm Gladwell is one of the best Thinkers of the twenty-first century. Interestingly, Gladwell is not a scientist, a CEO of a company, or a head coach, but a writer.

In 2005, *Time* magazine named Gladwell as one of the "100 Most Influential People." In researching how this New York writer came to write three blockbuster best sellers and have such a major influence on our views in these areas, I came across an interesting finding. Gladwell indicates that early in his career, he became heavily influenced by two social psychologists (much like the model in this book and like the model used by Charlie Munger). Their names are Richard Nisbett and Lee Ross, who together wrote the ground-breaking book, *The Person and the Situation*. Gladwell says this book changed his life and his worldview. This book has been a constant companion in all his writings. It describes how the context we are in influences the way we behave and the way we think. We are as much externally determined as internally determined! (Compare this idea to the concept of timing and context or culture in a person's life, as described throughout the previous chapters.)

THE SECRET TO EXTRAORDINARY SUCCESS:
BILL GATES AND THE 10,000-HOUR RULE

Gladwell interviewed gifted and successful individuals and found that while these individuals were smart and gifted, these traits were insufficient to account for their accomplishments. Geniuses aren't born; they are created, as there are plenty of high-IQ people who need to apply what he labeled the 10,000-hour rule. To demonstrate this, he focused on Bill Gates, the second-wealthiest individual in the world today.

When Gates was thirteen, he was sent to a private school that happened to have one of the only computers in the country on which students could do real-time programming. Then at age fifteen, he started to use the mainframe computer of the University of Washington, near his home, which was only available between 2:00 a.m. and 6:00 a.m. So Gates would get up at 1:30 in the morning and program for four hours. During seven months in 1971, he ran up 1,575 hours of computer time. By the time he dropped out of Harvard University after his sophomore year, he had clocked ten thousand programming hours, more programming time than all but a few people in the world!

Timing and particularly hard work were the critical factors that pointed to Gates's overall extraordinary success. This 10,000-hour rule is the main "outlier" to all the other behaviors that determine leadership greatness.

Energy often is more important than giftedness, intelligence, and other innate characteristics. A culture or context that allows you to practice these ten thousand hours (the equivalent of ten years at four hours per day) is crucial. The personality trait of "energy" can be found in almost every leader of a dynasty. It drives and magnifies each of the other eight personality traits. and often separates the great from the elite. In short, Gladwell is a big believer in energy as a leading personality trait for long-time leadership success.

MICROSOFT: AN EXAMPLE OF THE ENERGY TRAIT

What a remarkable story! How do you become the second-wealthiest man in the world? Easy—work hard! Bill Gates describes himself in childhood as a very stubborn young man with a lot of energy. It started in high school for "Trey" (his nickname) and his buddy Paul Allen as they started a number of small entrepreneurial projects. In 1975, he dropped out of Harvard to join Allen, who had been working for Honeywell, to develop the software for a company in Albuquerque that had just made the world's first personal computer. They knew instinctively that their window of opportunity (timing) was short. Gates did return to Harvard later to receive his honorary doctorate and give the commencement address.

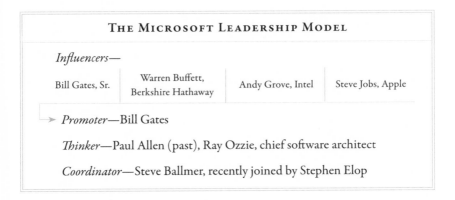

THE MICROSOFT LEADERSHIP MODEL			
Influencers—			
Bill Gates, Sr.	Warren Buffett, Berkshire Hathaway	Andy Grove, Intel	Steve Jobs, Apple

*Promoter—*Bill Gates

*Thinker—*Paul Allen (past), Ray Ozzie, chief software architect

*Coordinator—*Steve Ballmer, recently joined by Stephen Elop

Bill gates currently serves as chairman of this 90,000-employee company in 105 countries, with net income of $18 billion and $73 billion in assets.

TEAM-TO-DYNASTY TIP #25. Be like Warren—keep things simple! Warren's special genius that Bill Gates follows is to boil things down and work on things that matter by energetically thinking through the basics.

Steve Ballmer was in the same class at Harvard as Gates and lived in the same dorm hall. Intense and energetic as Gates, with a passion for business, he graduated from Harvard but dropped out of the Stanford Graduate School of Business to join Gates and Allen when they had only thirty staff members. Steve became the coordinator and business guru who allowed Bill to promote and think and Paul to think. Early on, Bill Gates had this vision of putting a computer on every desk, in every home—a phenomenon that has truly changed the world.

THE BILL AND MELINDA GATES FOUNDATION

Another common trait of dynasty leaders is energetic involvement in philanthropy. The Bill and Melinda Gates Foundation has over $60 billion in it, with all of Buffett's money ($40 billion more) to come over during the next ten to fifteen years. Bill and Melinda serve as Promoter and Thinker with former Microsoft star Jeff Raikes as the foundation's CEO, now in the Coordinator role.

HONORABLE MENTION: McDONALD'S

Like Gates an energetic and hardworking individual, Ray Kroc, in the mid-1950s, purchased the McDonald's chain, which had nine restaurants at the time. He instituted the franchise model and grew it to 31,000 locations worldwide, with 400,000 employees serving some 47 million customers. Yet his real legacy is the donation of billions to his foundation, which is building dozens of large community centers all over the country.

ENERGY AND MENTAL TOUGHNESS

TEAM-TO-DYNASTY TIP #26. "The difference is almost all mental. The top players just hate to lose. A champion hates to lose even more than she loves to win." —Chris Evert, International Tennis Hall of Fame

Buffett, Gates, Kroc, and the really superstar athletes all have this same passion, this energy that drives them to be the best. Two examples are below—one of how a coach can energize a team and an entire sport over decades; and the other of a person who used to be the most mentally tough competitor in the world before his "existential meltdown."

PAT SUMMITT—WOMEN'S BASKETBALL COACH, TENNESSEE

Pat Summitt became the Tennessee Lady Vols' basketball coach at the age of twenty-two in 1974. She has won eight NCAA Titles and had over a thousand wins, with an 80 percent winning record. She has been voted the eleventh best coach of all time and is the only female among the top fifty coaches in the world at all levels in all sports. In her book *Reach for the Summit*, she stated, "Tennessee wins because, in the end, our players feel they have worked too hard not to." She is also always looking for that edge. "We are constantly working to be more thorough, fit, and more knowledgeable." Her work ethic and intensity involve always looking for the psychological, physical, or tactical edge to win. In her emphasis on the psychological and mental aspects, she was way ahead of her peers. Players take psychological tests and meet with a sports psychologist; coaches embark on an ambitious self-improvement program in the off-season—all to get the most out of everyone.

I had the opportunity to work with the University of Tennessee's football coaching staff. They visited our program in the summer of 1998 after our Nebraska football team defeated them for the national championship in 1997. They had glowing praise for Coach Summitt, whom they described as really understanding the "mental game" perhaps better than any other coach in the country.

They duplicated many aspects of our program, including the Unity Council, and won the national championship the following season.

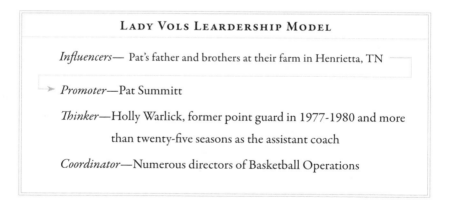

LADY VOLS LEARDERSHIP MODEL

Influencers— Pat's father and brothers at their farm in Henrietta, TN

Promoter—Pat Summitt

Thinker—Holly Warlick, former point guard in 1977-1980 and more than twenty-five seasons as the assistant coach

Coordinator—Numerous directors of Basketball Operations

Finally, how do you want to live your life? What will your legacy be? I have worked with many individuals who, when dying, have never said they wish they had more money or possessions, but almost all either cherish those who love them or regret that there were not more people to love them.

TIGER

Ever notice how the greatest players of sports in the world are often referred to with only one name—Pelé, Ali, Michael, Shaq, Babe, Peyton, and now perhaps the one person who most epitomized the mental toughness and energy it takes to be a true superstar: Tiger. There was not a better competitor in sports, particularly when he had to be, when the pressure was on. He could have won more tournaments than Sam Snead (82) and major championships than Jack Nicklaus (18) if he had continued on at his pace, and in a shorter period of time than all the greats—Ben Hogan, Arnold Palmer, and Nicklaus. His sheer athleticism was boosted by his devotion to fitness and the mental-toughness training he received from his father, Earl Woods.

Earl was the first African-American baseball player in the Big Eight conference, and he served two tours of duty in Vietnam as a Green Beret. He retired at the rank of colonel just before Tiger was born. Earl's mentorship and teaching techniques are found in his book, *Training a Tiger: A Father's Guide to Raising a Winner in Both Golf and Life* (1997).

He started teaching Tiger at age two and by the time he was eleven, he could beat his father, a good athlete. Tiger recalls being seven years old and playing on the Navy golf course with "Pop." His father would ask him where he wanted to hit the ball. Tiger would see a spot, and then his father would say, "Fine, go figure out how to do it." He taught his son to keep things simple, like Buffett and Sun Tzu and the other leaders mentioned, and to have that perfectionist passion, drive, and energy to persist. Tiger's model consists of his parents as Influencers, Earl as the Thinker, Tiger as the Promoter, and IMG and business agents as Coordinators. Tiger and Earl are one of the greatest father-son stories, serving as an inspiration for all mentor-mentee relationships. Perhaps Tiger's personal downfall started some five years before with the death of his father.

It is equally important to study unsuccessful leaders to see why they failed, because it reinforces the importance of all four components of the Championship Formula.

The essence of the Energy trait is best depicted by the greatest hockey player of all time. "I don't go where the puck is; I go where the puck will be," said Wayne Gretzky.

LAWS AND RULES

There are laws that govern our civilization; they help us function in an orderly manner. The rules, as adopted by organizations and teams, help us succeed by following these laws and avoiding negative consequences. Leaders who want to lead a company, a team, a church, a school, or any organization must adopt, implement, and enforce the rules to achieve the stated goals in a unified manner. Those who are most successful identify a personal set of rules of how to live their lives and how they treat others. People can be honest, analytical, resilient, etc., but if they don't consistently follow the rules themselves or fail to identify and reinforce the ethical guidelines in their own behavior, they will find their goals to be elusive. As Mark Twain said, "Always do what is right. This will gratify some, and astonish the rest."

BUFFETT ON ENERGY AND RULES TO LIVE BY

Warren employs 250,000 individuals in his companies, but only nineteen individuals work at the Berkshire Hathaway headquarters in Omaha. He puts in long hours each day and has no plans to retire soon. His energy inspires us all. Warren could do or own just about anything. He would not have to follow ethical guidelines, work hard anymore, or lead a structured lifestyle. Yet he owns no yachts. There are no big security gates at his unpretentious corner lot in an older but modest neighborhood in central Omaha. His home is the house he purchased more than fifty years ago for $31,500. He states that he lives better than John D. Rockefeller did in his days. He has already left 95 percent of his life's earnings to the Bill and Melinda Gates Foundation. That's right—he amassed the largest or second-largest body of wealth in the world and is donating it to someone else's foundation—a foundation without his name on it. That says it all about how he lives his life and why companies today want to be associated with him—it's instant credibility.

PERFORMANCE ENHANCEMENT PLAN

I have found, particularly in consulting to executives and coaches in my practice, that the annual development of a performance plan designed to enhance the key areas of one's life works wonders in guiding individuals to a successful lifestyle. There are seven rules to live by that I have found necessary for a long-term personal winning formula. I have successfully used this plan with hundreds of leaders at the top who embrace the comprehensiveness of this plan.

HEALTH

Confucius was once asked, "What surprises you most about mankind?" He answered, "They lose their health to make money and then lose their money to restore their health. By thinking anxiously about the future, they forget the present, such that they live neither for the present nor the future and they live as if they will never die, and they die as if they had never lived."

It's difficult to be a leader if you are absent or your health restricts your performance. I am always amazed (as much as old Confucius) by how little people know about their own health and by their reluctance to seek excellent medical care. I often ask people their golf score, bowling score, etc., and they know the answer. But most can't tell me their blood pressure, cholesterol levels, and other vital scores. They may not even get regular health checkups or see a physician on a regular basis. I even use guilt as a way to prod them—"Be there for your grandkids or loved ones, people need you." Stress levels are so high today (directly linked to 80 percent of all doctor office visits, with 43 percent of the population exhibiting burn-out symptoms) that the incidence of health disorders such as diabetes, heart, cancer, and depression is alarmingly high despite the vast knowledge and treatment procedures available today.

FAMILY

As mentioned previously, having someone to love and who loves you in return not only enriches life but also prolongs it, according to research. Those who are happily married and have a close relationship with their kids or extended family consistently rated higher on happiness scores, and they live an average of three years longer. Unfortunately, recent research by the National Center for Health Statistics found that 40 percent of all births today are now to unwed mothers, either by choice or circumstance. This is a stunning statistic with profound implications for future winning championship teams, let alone dynasties.

SUPPORT SYSTEMS

Quality friends, coworkers, and neighbors all contribute to an essential "support-system rule to live by," as they bring us enormous amounts of joy and happiness. Working with quality people and having a friend at work is the top factor in what people want in a job today—compensation ranks fifth. Personal surveys of my patients and other research (Lyubomirsky 2008) indicates that people rate components of personal happiness in this order: (1) family, (2) health, (3) personal accomplishments, (4) friends, and (5) money. Individuals with terminal diseases live longer with a support system or have even less health problems to begin with. Friends are like buttons—they hold us together. Khalil Gibran best captured the importance of friendship in a few lines: "For what is your friend that you should seek him with hours to kill? Seek him always with hours to live. For it is his to fill your need, but not your emptiness."

ACTIVITIES AND HOBBIES OF HAPPINESS

Happiness doesn't just happen—one has to work at it. Pursuing activities and hobbies that bring you happiness will give you the capacity to allow others to plug into your energy and draw their support from you. But you also need to conserve, learn how to say no, and save enough time for your own renewal.

The level of happiness that is in our power to control is a surprising 40 percent, based on the research of Sonja Lyubomirsky. Her prize-winning research over two decades indicates that positive self-feedback and self-talks can greatly sustain one's happiness-index scores. Additional research findings indicate that we as a country are less happy than we were in the 1950s. People become happier as they get older, and the difference in happiness levels between wealthy people and the community that Mother Teresa served in Calcutta is not that significant; we all learn to adapt. A Lou Harris poll in 2008 indicated that only 51 percent of people are very happy, 41 percent are somewhat happy, and only 9 percent are very unhappy. Iceland ranks number one in happiness, the United States is in the high average, and India and the Dominican Republic rank statistically unhappy.

JOB SKILLS AND GROWTH

It is my experience that in the world of work today it is not how much you are paid, where you work, what you do at work, but who is your immediate boss that impacts an individual's work happiness the most. Sadly, only a third of the workforce are happy with their jobs today. Research of the top one hundred companies to work for found that happy workers are highly correlated with companies' profitability. It pays to treat employees and teammates well. Job satisfaction is the most important factor for individuals and has a profound impact on their daily well-being and that of their families.

People want and need psychological well-being and are fearful of change or unpredictable events. They worry about losing their jobs, their homes, and their lifestyle. That's why having a vision of the future is so important and why having a boss who guides and supports you in that journey is so critical. Finding supervisors, managers, leaders, or coaches with these skills is now more important than ever.

I always recommend to individuals that, if possible, they make backup plans and have other job offers in case something happens to their current job—it gives them security even if they choose not to exercise these options.

Everyone should have a short-term and long-term job-skills plan that includes timelines on how to acquire these skills. This training can be personal or formal, but is important for long-term success and avoidance of stagnation.

ALTRUISTIC SERVICES

Mentoring is one of the important altruistic services—either giving or receiving—that impact people's lives. Research once again indicates that the happiest people are also the most giving. This history of taking care of others is built into our anthropological DNA from very early civilizations in which the older, wiser, and more experienced, but often fragile, members of a tribe were taken care of by the younger members, and both benefited from this survival process.

Today there is a high correlation between very successful companies and teams and leaders of such companies who are philanthropic by nature. It is not an accident that the two wealthiest individuals in the world— Gates and Buffett—will give away almost all of their accumulated assets to the Bill and Melinda Gates Foundation. They are also challenging other billionaires to pledge half their wealth to charity before they pass away. Almost every high-profile coach in every sport appears to be dedicated to a special charity.

All of us should identify an altruistic endeavor to become involved in, as it helps us to keep our balance psychologically while keeping life in perspective—a prerequisite for all of the CHARACTER traits.

John Mackey, the cofounder and CEO of Whole Foods Market, believes that the 2008–2010 recession forever changed our behavior regarding the pursuit of corporate profits. He advocates for what he refers to as "conscious capitalism," in which each organization is about more than just making money. Leadership should serve the enterprise and its stakeholders. Coaches who pursue wins only to advance themselves don't last long, or the team quickly finds that they are being used. Mackey says that entrepreneurs are not averse to making money, but that few ever start a business only to make money. They usually have some big idea that really ignites their creative spirits. Bill Gates and Warren Buffett were motivated more by the exciting idea of a contributing to society than the pursuit of maximum wealth.

SPIRITUALITY

Ah, but a man's reach should exceed his grasp or what's a Heaven for?.
—Robert Browning

Lastly, the happiest people and frequently most successful individuals believe in something bigger than themselves, a higher power—something to live for, by and within, guiding them, a goal throughout their lives.

In 2009, religious leaders, including Pope Benedict XVI, spoke out about the need for companies to act responsibly in the global economy and consider the impact on employees and society. The Dalai Lama encouraged companies and leaders to act in accordance with the Buddhist principles of "right conduct" and "right view."

For individuals a life based on spiritual principles is a powerful statement to others. What you say may attract great admiration, but it can set you up for unforgiving backlash if what you do doesn't match it.

People remember

» 10 percent of what we read

» 20 percent of what we hear

» 30 percent of what we see

» 50 percent of what we both see and hear

» 70 percent of what we both say and write

» 90 percent of what we and others DO

There are fundamental rules to living a happy and successful life. Failure to take care of each of these seven areas—health, family, support systems, hobbies, job skills, altruistic services, and spirituality—will eventually catch up to a person and prevent him or her from reaching ultimate goals.

The pursuit of true happiness is the common thread among all these areas of the performance enhancement plan. The happiest people take care of their health, and their health is better because of their relationships with their family and a sound support system.

A FINAL BLESSING

The pursuit of all these rules contribute to a significant boost in the length and quality of life.

> *May the road rise up to meet you,*
> *May the wind be always at your back,*
> *May the sun shine warm upon your face,*
> *The rains fall soft upon your fields, and until we meet again,*
> *May God hold you in the palm of His hand.*
> *—An Irish blessing*

Take this blessing and this formula for building a team into a dynasty with you on your journey. Take this model and post it near you as a reminder of what it takes to win in life.

It's like baking a large wedding cake. The cake is an essential part of every wedding, just as a formula to follow is necessary for life's challenges. Some cakes are more elaborate with lots of layers. Some taste better, look better, and last longer.

The key is who is baking the cake, their skills, the proper timing of baking, the key ingredients, and the process of adding them. And last, the purpose of the cake—to look good and taste good.

If you skip some ingredients, take shortcuts in the process, have inexperienced people involved, or the timing is off, you can wind up with a half-baked disaster.

However, when everything comes together for that perfect result, you have a winning formula, a winning team, and a dominating dynasty that you and others will never forget.

See you at the podium!

FROM TEAM-TO-DYNASTY TIPS

TEAM-TO-DYNASTY TIP #1. It is four times harder and takes four times as long to build a successful dynasty as it does to destroy one.

TEAM-TO-DYNASTY TIP #2. By studying the people who mentored and shaped a leader, you learn a great deal about the essence of a championship leader.

TEAM-TO-DYNASTY TIP #3. Be aware of the stage of moral development of both yourself and of those leaders you choose to follow.

TEAM-TO-DYNASTY TIP #4. You can easily judge the character of a man by the way he treats those who can do nothing for him.

TEAM-TO-DYNASTY TIP #5. "Character cannot be developed in ease and quiet. Only through experience of trial and suffering can the soul be strengthened, vision cleared, ambition inspired and success achieved." —Helen Keller

TEAM-TO-DYNASTY TIP #6. The guiding principle in our quest for happiness is our instinct for self-preservation, which concerns our ability to be secure and to predict that this security will continue.

TEAM-TO-DYNASTY TIP #7. The person at the top will determine the personality or culture of an entire civilization, country, company, or team.

TEAM-TO-DYNASTY TIP #8. "The first and last thing required of genius is the love of truth." —Goethe

TEAM-TO-DYNASTY TIP #9. "A sense of humor can help you overlook the unattractive, tolerate the unpleasant, cope with the unexpected and smile through the unbearable." —Moshe Waldoks

TEAM-TO-DYNASTY TIP #10. "Be more concerned with your character than with your reputation, because your character is what you really are, while your reputation is merely what others think you are." (John Wooden). People will question you or criticize you and there will be times you even may doubt yourself. But if you take care of your character, maintain a positive attitude through the tough times, your dynasty will prevail.

TEAM-TO-DYNASTY TIP #11. "Success is peace of mind, which is a direct result of self-satisfaction in knowing you made the effort to do the best of which you are capable." —John Wooden

TEAM-TO-DYNASTY TIP #12. "Winning is an attitude . . . and the attitude of the leader of the pack usually determines the speed of the pack!" —Phil Jackson.

TEAM-TO-DYNASTY TIP #13. Never underestimate the depth and level some people will stoop to to disparage your reputation, if they are envious of your accomplishment or the position you espouse. Every great leader will have detractors. Evil exists in human nature and when others cannot defeat you, they may spread rumors or attack your character. Don't stoop to their insecure, petty level. Simply outlast them.

TEAM-TO-DYNASTY TEAM TIP #14. "A man may die, nations may rise and fall, but an idea lives on." —John F. Kennedy

TEAM-TO-DYNASTY TIP #15. Warren Buffett's philosophy: Rule #1— Never lose money. Rule #2—Never forget Rule #1.

TEAM-TO-DYNASTY TIP #16. When handling a crisis, make your mantra: Go fast! Go hard! Go long!

TEAM-TO-DYNASTY TIP #17. "The single most important ingredient in the 'formula of success' is knowing how to get along with people." —Theodore Roosevelt.

TEAM-TO-DYNASTY TIP #18. The key to being a great leader or coach is the ability to treat your team equally, but each individual differently based on their unique personality. (We all love our children the same, yet differently based on their personality.)

TEAM-TO-DYNASTY TIP #19. The best time to make a major cultural team change is when there has been a crisis or failure. People are more open to trying something new.

TEAM-TO-DYNASTY TIP #20. Timing and context are everything. Know when to get in and know when to get out! Life is timing. As that Kenny Rogers song goes—"You have to know when to hold them and know when to fold them."

TEAM-TO-DYNASTY TIP #21. The difference of 5 percent in winning or ROI can be the difference between a mediocre team and a national championship team.

TEAM-TO-DYNASTY TIP #22. Truman wasn't afraid to have people around him who were more accomplished than he. That's one reason why he had the best cabinet of any president since George Washington.

TEAM-TO-DYNASTY TIP #23. One of the biggest challenges in molding and keeping a winning team is in selecting and developing talented people. The key is to have a leadership training-and-development process that changes leaders' behavior and perpetuates winning.

TEAM-TO-DYNASTY TIP #24. To be kind to all, to like many and love a few, to be needed and wanted by those we love is certainly the nearest we can come to happiness. —Mary Roberts Rinehart

TEAM-TO-DYNASTY TIP #25. Be like Warren—keep things simple! Warren's special genius that Bill Gates follows is to boil things down and work on things that matter by energetically thinking through the basics.

TEAM-TO-DYNASTY TIP #26. "The difference is almost all mental. The top players just hate to lose. A champion hates to lose even more than she loves to win," —Chris Evert, International Tennis Hall of Fame

Behavioral Assessment & Selection Survey (b.a.s.s.)

Today, more than ever, every single hiring decision is a critical decision. The B.A.S.S. uses the latest research findings by utilizing the behavioral interviewing process, which is designed to minimize surface impressions that can affect the hiring decision. When you focus on the applicant's actions and behaviors, rather than subjective impressions (which can sometimes be misleading) the interviewer(s) can make a more accurate hiring decision.

SELECTION ERRORS

The B.A.S.S. is designed to avoid the selection errors that can create a bad fit and a legally indefensible selection decision. In interviews you should make every effort to avoid

- » Accepting vague answers
- » Leading or telegraphing what answer you may be looking for
- » Talking too much or getting sidetracked
- » Relying on your memory instead of written notes

» Making subjective, snap judgments based on your gut feelings

» Showing biases that impact the interview process

» Making any reference to age, gender, race, religion, color, or disability

» Being swayed by people who can con you in an interview

» Hiring people whom you think you know but don't

» Assuming skills and talents based on a puffed-up resume

STEPS OF INTERVIEWING

STEP I—THE OPENING

Greet and establish rapport. Put the candidate at ease. This usually consists of shaking hands and an ice-breaker comment—weather, how the interviews are going, whether they would like a cup of coffee.

Explain the B.A.S.S. process in order to immediately take charge and structure the process in a timely manner.

Verify resume data—check for accuracy and "puffing." Remember, past behavior is the best indicator of future behavior.

Let the candidate know you will be taking notes and why.

Give the candidate an idea of about how long the interview will last.

Explain that you need honest, accurate information and that, since no one is perfect, it's also helpful to know when the candidate has been disappointed in jobs past.

STEP II—THE BEHAVIORAL ASSESSMENT & SELECTION SURVEY

This is the meat of the interview process, where you want to determine whether a good fit exists for this candidate based upon the predetermined success characteristics.

STEP III—INFORMATION EXCHANGE

This is an open-ended exchange of information in which the candidate may want to ask additional questions or in which you may ask for any additional information that would be helpful to know about the candidate.

STEP IV—THE CLOSING

Let the candidate know the follow-up process of how, when and where they will be contacted regarding a hiring decision. Close with a positive exchange.

B.A.S.S. RATING INDEX
1–2 = Skill level at the lower 10% of candidates.
3–4 = Skill level at the 10–40% range of candidates.
5–6 = Skill level at the 40–60% range of candidates.
7–8 = Skill level at the 60–90% range of candidates.
9–10 = Skill level at the top 10% of candidates

RATING THE CANDIDATE

WORK ETHIC

A long history of working hard, getting the task accomplished, on time and with high standards. This standard of excellence also inspires others to perform with high energy and a responsibility for their outcome.

2	4	6	8	10

LEADERSHIP

The ability to persuade others to set aside for a period of time their individual concerns and pursue a common goal that is important and good for the company or team.

2	4	6	8	10

INTERPERSONAL SKILLS

An ability to connect with others, understand and react to their thoughts and feelings, and develop a relationship of trust.

2	4	6	8	10

COMMUNICATION—CONFLICT MANAGEMENT

The ability to speak, to write, to listen, and to interpret information in an effective manner. An ability to handle conflict.

2	4	6	8	10

INTEGRITY–PROFESSIONALISM

The ability to behave in an ethical manner; core values, honesty, and respect are recognized in daily actions.

2	4	6	8	10

PROBLEM SOLVING

An ability to make decisions based upon analyzing problems, thinking creatively, and using wisdom, judgment, and common sense after carefully reviewing complex information in an objective manner.

2	4	6	8	10

ORGANIZATION–ATTENTION TO DETAIL

The ability to handle multiple tasks, store and retrieve information, prioritize, remain consistent, and be on time with people and attend to detail.

2	4	6	8	10

ATTITUDE–DEALING WITH THE HIGHS & LOWS

The ability to keep going despite setbacks, time demands, conflicts, and rejections while standing by decisions despite second guessing and disagreement from others. Ability to deal with the highs and lows.

2	4	6	8	10

JOB SKILLS–RESOURCEFULNESS

The ability to maximize resources of time, staff, finances, and information to assure success. Job flexibility and attention to detail. An ability to follow policies and procedures.

2	4	6	8	10

JOB COMMITMENT

Dedication, loyalty, and a willingness to work with this company. Is this a career path the candidate wants to be on in the long term?

2	4	6	8	10

TOTAL SCORE

Behavioral Assessment & Selection Survey (B.A.S.S.) _____

SAMPLE QUESTIONS

LEADERSHIP

The ability to persuade others to set aside for a period of time their individual concerns and pursue a common goal that is important and good for the company.

Give examples of when you succeeded and failed in a leadership role and what you learned from it. _____

_____

_____

What experience in your past jobs is most reflective of your leadership ability? _____

_____

What is your philosophy of managing others and how do you want to be managed? _____

_____

Give some examples of people you admire as leaders and tell us why. _____

_____

_____

Are you a role model for others? How do you get people to follow you?

_____

_____

INTERPERSONAL SKILLS

An ability to connect with others, understand and react to their thoughts and feelings, and develop a relationship of trust.

How would you describe your personality? _____

_____

_____

How would a friend describe your personality? _____

_____

_____

How would a person who doesn't like you describe your personality? _____

_____

_____

What are your strengths and weaknesses with people? _____

_____

_____

How would you describe a person who has great "people skills" and why?

_____

_____

Do you have the people skills to be a successful person at this company?

_____

_____

Explain how you are able to connect with people, understand and react to
their needs, and thereby develop a trusting relationship with them. _____

_____

_____

ACKNOWLEDGMENTS

Wow! What an incredible journey I have been blessed to experience. More than thirty years of experience in both the business community and the sports world. It's time! It's time to share these experiences with others so that they may benefit as much as I have from so many remarkable relationships.

The sports world has been my passion and has brought me so much joy. Interestingly, with the exception of NASCAR, I have never made any money in sports. I always considered it a privilege to make presentations to schools, churches and community groups, athletes and coaches. I can point to one person whom I have been incredibly privileged to work with for over twenty years, an extraordinary man, Dr. Tom Osborne. As the team psychologist for the Nebraska Huskers with him, from 1989 to 2003, I learned the essence of building a championship team—a dynasty in the 1990s with three national championships. Thank you, Tom. His successor, Frank Solich, the greatest running-backs coach in this history of college football and a man who never got the credit he deserved, also remains a close friend. I have also cherished my twenty-five years with

Coach Mike Denney, former head wrestling coach at UNO and winner of eight national championships, and fourteen years with Mike Kemp, former head hockey coach at UNO. There are dozens of other coaches at some thirty colleges and pro teams in multiple sports that I have benefited from also. I have particularly enjoyed these last six years at Creighton University with athletic director Bruce Rasmussen and head basketball coach Greg McDermott.

The last eleven years, I have also been privileged to work with Rick Hendrick at Hendrick Motorsports. He is a remarkable man who has won over two hundred races in twenty-six years and a dozen championships and is now recognized as part of the best dynasty in the history of all motorsports. It isn't just what he has accomplished but also his charisma and caring that distinguish him. I owe him a huge debt for allowing me to be a part of this wonderful journey. My friendship and relationship with one his former drivers—Brian Vickers—is very, very special to me. While I have been fortunate to work with some of the top athletes in the world who have achieved the highest honors, Brian stands out above them all. He is the most remarkable athlete I have ever had the opportunity to work with. We have particularly enjoyed our relationship with his parents, Clyde and Ramona, our good friends.

The more than three hundred former and current pro athletes I've worked with are like sons who have brought extraordinary happiness to my life. I was also privileged to see over ten thousand clients in my private practice all of whom have tremendously enriched my life.

In my consulting work with the business community, I have learned much from many companies. I particularly appreciate the friendship, support, and resilience of David Sokol and his entire family. I have also benefited from a great friendship with the CEO of a local public utility— Gary Gates, Omaha Public Power District. Hundreds of other CEOs, VPs, and senior staff have taught me a great deal about leadership and what it takes to make a good team into a dynasty.

I want to also acknowledge a number of my lifelong friends who have been active in services for the disabled, especially my former mentor Dr. Frank Menolascino and his entire family, as well as the AAIDD—American Association on Intellectual & Developmental Disabilities—a very dedicated and altruistic group of people who helped our family cope. A special appreciation goes to Mosaic, a national service provider to some five thousand individuals who are developmentally disabled. Mosaic took exceptional care of our son John, and for this, we would like to donate all proceeds from this book to their foundation. Bob Schalock, a lifelong friend who spent a great deal of time in mentoring me in this endeavor, also deserves credit.

To all of you, I deeply acknowledge your influence and appreciate your support.

If I have been able to see farther than others,
it is because I have stood on the shoulders of giants.
—Sir Isaac Newton

Notes

INTRODUCTION

Collins, Jim (2001). *Good to Great: Why Some Companies Make the Leap... and Others Don't*. NYC: HarperCollins Publishers, Inc.

Lencioni, Patrick (2002). *The Five Dysfunctions of a Team: A Leadership Fable*. San Francisco: Jossey-Bass.

Sayles, Leonard and Cynthia Smith (2005). *The Rise of the Rogue Executive: How Good Companies Go Bad and How to Stop the Destruction*. Prentice Hall.

Anderson, Odin (1975). *Blue Cross Since 1929: Accountability and the Public Trust*. Cambridge: Ballinger Publishing Company.

Van Vugt, Mark, Robert Hogan, and Robert Kaiser (2008). "Leadership, Followership and Evolution: Some Lessons from the Past." American Psychologist, 63, 182–196.

Bono, J.J. (2004). "Personality and Transformational and Transactional Leadership: A Meta-Analysis." Journal of Applied Psychology, Vol. 89, No 5, pp. 901–910.

Warren, Rick (2002). *The Purpose Driven Life.* Grand Rapids: Zondervan.

Drucker, Peter (2001). *The Essential Drucker: In One Volume the Best of Sixty Years of Peter Drucker's Essential Writings on Management.* NYC: HarperCollins Publishers, Inc.

Bennis, Warren (1989). *Why Leaders Can't Lead.* Jossey Bass.

Crocker III, H.W. (1999). *Robert E. Lee on Leadership: Executive Lessons in Character, Courage, and Vision.* Roseville: Prima Publishing.

Carrison, Dan and Rod Walsh (1999). *Semper Fi: Business Leadership the Marine Corps Way.* NYC: Amacom.

Osborne, Tom (1985). *More than Winning.* Thomas Nelson, Inc.

Krzyzewski, Mike (2001). *Leading with the Heart: Coach K's Successful Strategies for Basketball, Business and Life.* Business Plus/Warner Books.

Dungy, Tony (2007). *Quiet Strength: The Principles, Practices and Priorities of a Winning Life.* Illinois: Tyndale House.

CHAPTER I

Mayo, Anthony (2005). *In Their Time.* Boston: Harvard Business School Press.

CHAPTER 2

Kohlberg, Lawrence and Charles Levine (1983). *Moral Stages: A Current Formulation and a Response to Critics.* Basel, NY: Karger.

CHAPTER 3

Kotter, John (1999). *What Leaders Really Do*. Boston: Harvard School Business Press.

Schein, Ed (1999). *The Corporate Culture Survival Guide*. San Francisco: Jossey-Bass.

CHAPTER 4

World Health Organization (2011). United Nations. http://www.who.int/en/

Maraniss, David (1999). *When Pride Still Mattered: A Life of Vince Lombardi*. Simon & Schuster.

Reilly, Rick (2000, March 20). "A Paragon Rising Above the Madness". Sports Illustrated.

Wooden, John (2004). *My Personal Best: Life Lessons from an All-American Journey*. McGraw-Hill.

Forbes (2008, January 7).

Jackson, Phil (1995). *Sacred Hoops: Spiritual Lessons of a Hardwood Warrior*. NYC: Hyperion.

Phillips, Donald (1992). *Lincoln on Leadership*. NYC: Warner Books.

CHAPTER 5

Kipling, Rudyard (1894). The Jungle Book.

Martin, Roger (2007). *How Successful Leaders Think*. Harvard Business Review.

Martin, Roger (2007). *The Opposable Mind: How Successful Leaders Win Through Integrative Thinking.* Harvard Business School Press.

Reingold, Jennifer (2008, November 24th). "Meet Your New Leaders." *Fortune*, pp. 145–146.

Charan, Ram (2009). *Leadership in the Era of Economic Uncertainty: The New Rules for Getting the Right Things Done in Difficult Times.* McGraw-Hill.

Morris, Betsy (2008, March 17). "What Makes Apple Golden". *Fortune*, p 68.

Bevelin, Peter (2007). *Seeking Wisdom: From Darwin to Munger.* Malmo, Sweden: PCA Publications.

Munger, Charles (1995). "A Lesson on Elementary, Worldly Wisdom As It Relates to Investment Management Business." Outstanding Investor Digest, pp. 49–63.

Munger, Charles (2005). *Poor Charlie's Alamnack.* Donning Company Publishers.

CHAPTER 6

Gartner, John (2009, July 1). *Field Guide to the Hypomanic: Hothead of State.* Psychology Today, pp. 36–38.

Hauser, Thomas (2004). *Muhammad Ali: His Life and Times.* Robin Books.

Goleman, Daniel, Richard Boyatzis, and Annie McKee (2002). *Primal Leadership: Realizing the Power of Emotional Intelligence.* Harvard Business Press.

Bradberry, Travis and Jean Greaves (2005). *The Emotional Intelligence Quick Book: Everything You Need to Know to Put Your EQ to Work.* New York: Simon & Schuster.

Cooper, Robert and Ayman Sawaf (1996). *Executive EQ: Emotional Intelligence in Leadership and Organizations.* Gosset/Putnam.

CHAPTER 7

Sokol, David (2007). *Pleased But Not Satisfied.* Self-Published.

Bossidy, Lawrence and Ram Charon (2002). *Execution: The Discipline of Getting Things Done.* Crown Business.

American Psychiatric Association (1994). *The Diagnostic and Statistical Manual of Mental Disorders*, 4th Edition.

Welch, Jack (2005). *Winning.* NYC: HarperCollins Publishers, Inc.

Babb, Kent (2009, April 19th). "NFL Teams Examine Minds as Well as Bodies of Potential Draft Picks." *The Kansas City Star.*

CHAPTER 8

Osborne, Tom (1999). *Faith in the Game: Lessons on Football, Work and Life.* Broadway Books.

USA Today (2008, June 19). p. 7C.

CHAPTER 9

Skinner, Burrhus Frederic (1953). *The Science of Human Behavior*. Harvard Press.

Covey, Stephen (1990). *The Seven Habits of Highly Effective People*. Free Press.

CHAPTER 10

Frankl, Viktor (1959). *Man's Search for Meaning*.

Levinson, Daniel (1978). *The Seasons of a Man's Life*. NYC: Knopf.

CHAPTER 11

Gladwell, Malcolm (2008). *Outliers: The Story of Success*. Little Brown.

Gladwell, Malcolm (2005). *Blink: The Power of Thinking Without Thinking*. Little, Brown & Co.

Cialdini, Robert (2001). *Influence: Science and Practice* (4th Edition). Boston: Allyn & Bacon.

Cialdini, Robert (1984). *Influence: The Psychology of Persuasion*. NYC.

Ross, Lee and Richard Nisbett (1991). *The Person and the Situation: Perspectives of Social Psychology*. Philadelphia: Temple University Press.

Facella, Paul (2008). *Everything I Know About Business I Learned at McDonald's: The 7 Leadership Principles that Drive Breakout Success*. McGraw Hill.

Summitt, Pat (2000). *Reach for the Summit*. McGraw Hill.

Woods, Earl (1997). *Training a Tiger: A Father's Guide to Raising a Winner in Both Golf and Life*. William Morrow.

Duplacey, James and Dan Diamond (1998). *Total Hockey: The Official Encyclopedia of the NHL*. Total Sports.

Hajek, Heather (2009, March 1). *Large Increase in Unwed Mothers Around the World*. Health News.

Lyubomirsky, Sonja (2008). *The How of Happiness: A Scientific Approach to Getting the Life You Want*. Penguin Books.

INDEX

ABOUT THE AUTHOR

 As a performance psychologist, Jack Stark provides psychological and performance enhancement training to elite athletes at the collegiate, professional and Olympic levels. He served as the team psychologist (1989-2004) for the University of Nebraska Cornhusker football program. During his tenure Nebraska won 88% of its games including 3 national championships and had the highest winning percentage in the 1990s. He is in his 11th year as the team psychologist for NASCAR's premier Hendrick Motorsports Team (winner of 5 straight national championships). He maintains a practice as a licensed clinical psychologist and has provided assistance to more than 10,000 individuals. He served on the faculty of the Nebraska Medical Center's Departments of Psychiatry and Pediatrics as a tenured professor of medical psychology. He is founder and director of Performance Enhancement Group and consults to F-500 executives. He has made over 1,000 presentations on Leadership and Teamwork. Married 41 years, the Starks have three children John (deceased), Nick and Suzy.